AF521712

CHINESE CERAMICS

from the collection of

The Baltimore Museum of Art

Frances Klapthor

This project was supported by a grant from the National Endowment for the Arts; and through support from Eleanor K. Levy (Mrs. Lester S. Levy), and from the Museum's Julius Levy Memorial Fund.

Design: Claude Skelton
Photographs: Duane Suter

Cover: Cat. no. 24. Jin *Vase.*
BMA 1990.156.

Library of Congress Cataloging-in-Publication Data

Baltimore Museum of Art.
Chinese ceramics from the collection of the Baltimore Museum of Art / Frances Klapthor.
p. cm.
Cover title: Chinese ceramics, the Baltimore Museum of Art.
Includes bibliographical references.
ISBN 0-912298-65-0
1. Pottery, Chinese—Catalogs. 2. Porcelain, Chinese—Catalogs. 3. Pottery—Maryland—Baltimore—Catalogs. 4. Porcelain—Maryland—Baltimore—Catalogs. 5. Baltimore Museum of Art—Catalogs. I. Klapthor, Frances, 1956– . II. Title. III. Title: Chinese ceramics, the Baltimore Museum of Art.
NK4165.B28 1992
738'.0951'0747526—dc20 92-43490
CIP

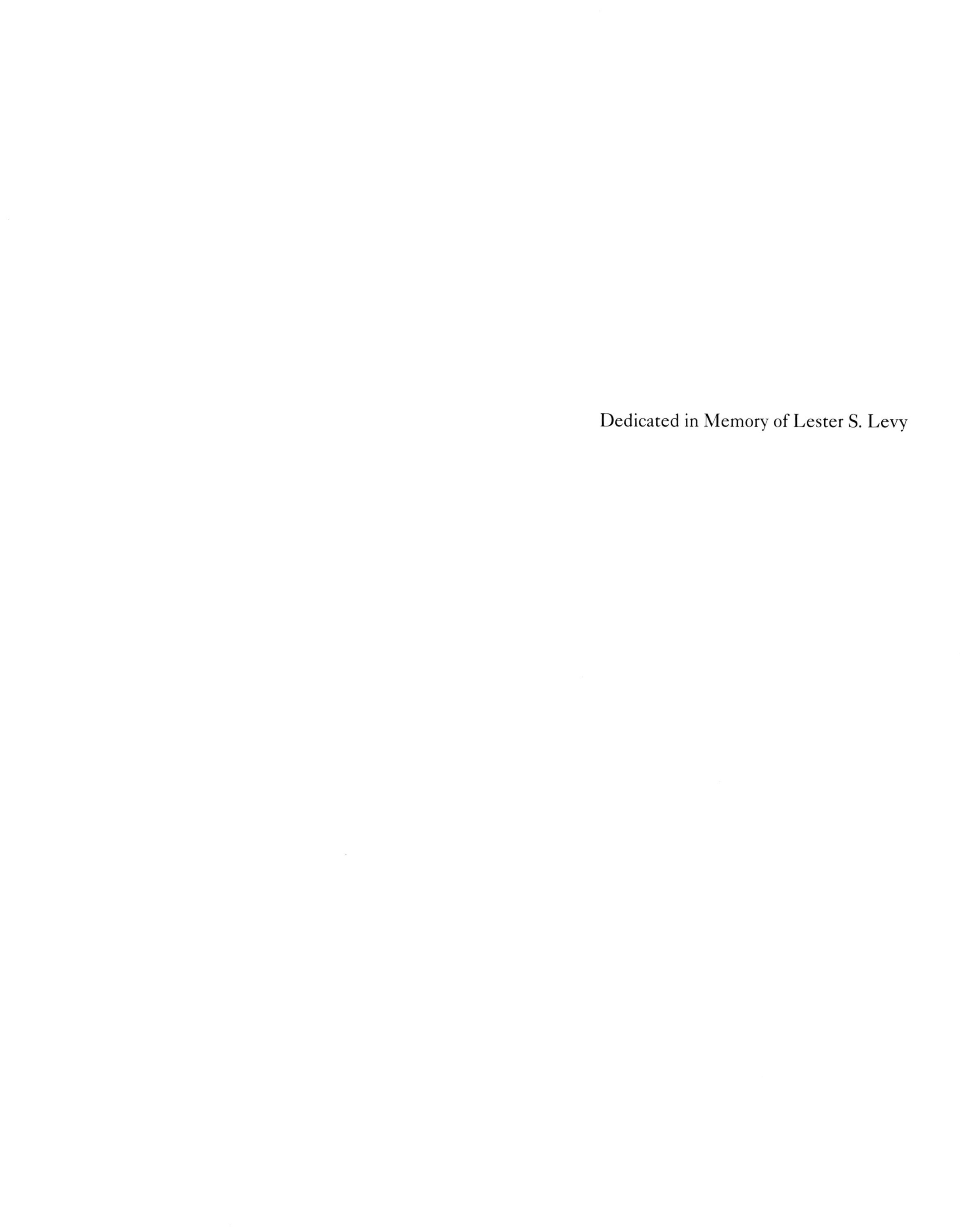

Dedicated in Memory of Lester S. Levy

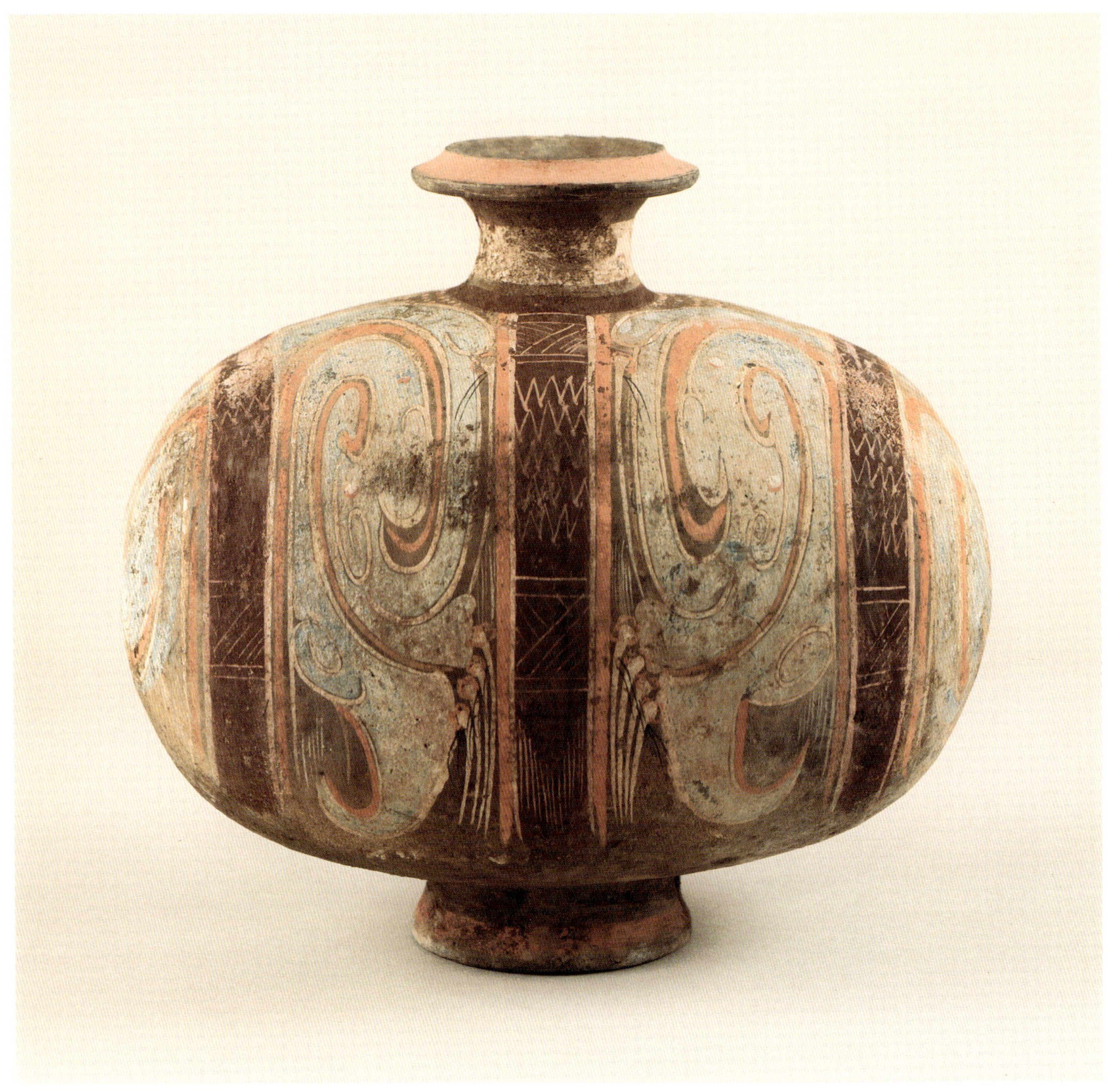

Western Han *Cocoon-form Jar*. BMA 1992.212; see p. 52.

ACKNOWLEDGMENTS

It is a privilege to introduce the Museum's first publication documenting its permanent collection of Asian art. In 1929—the year the Museum opened to the public in its new John Russell Pope building in Wyman Park—Ralph Chait gave a magnificent large storage jar that was the foundation of what would grow over the ensuing six decades into an unusually focused holding of Chinese ceramics with a special strength in earlier stonewares.

Over the last ten years the Asian collection has been developed and refined under the guidance of Frances Klapthor, the Museum's Associate Curator in Charge of the Arts of Asia. With initiative and careful research, strategic vision, and a remarkable eye, she has brought into the collection some of its most beautiful and important pieces and has, at the same time, expanded awareness of the collection among both specialists and the public. Ms. Klapthor has prepared this catalogue with the same professionalism and commitment that she brings to every aspect of her curatorial responsibilities and, on behalf of the Trustees, we extend to her our admiration and gratitude.

Publication of *Chinese Ceramics from the Collection of The Baltimore Museum of Art* is supported with the Museum's Julius Levy Memorial Fund. Mrs. Lester Levy, who consistently demonstrates her dedication to all aspects of the Museum's programming in the Arts of Asia, generously provided additional support, for which we are extremely grateful. And finally, a grant from the National Endowment for the Arts made much-needed matching funds available to realize the publication project.

Publication of *Chinese Ceramics* was a demanding team effort. Cecilia Meisner, Development Associate, organized and monitored the funding effort. Audrey Frantz, Director of Publications, and Lisa Pupa, Publications Assistant, managed the book's production with their usual dedication and meticulous attention to detail. And Brenda Richardson, Deputy Director for Art, provided administrative oversight of every phase of the project, working closely with Frances Klapthor from the outset on the book's conception and format.

Finally, I want to acknowledge our Board of Trustees, under the current leadership of Chairman James S. Riepe, for its commitment to the importance of publication of the Museum's permanent collection. We proudly add *Chinese Ceramics* to a distinguished library of collection publications that we hope serve as substantive reference to specialists and as a source of beauty and discovery for the public.

Arnold L. Lehman
Director

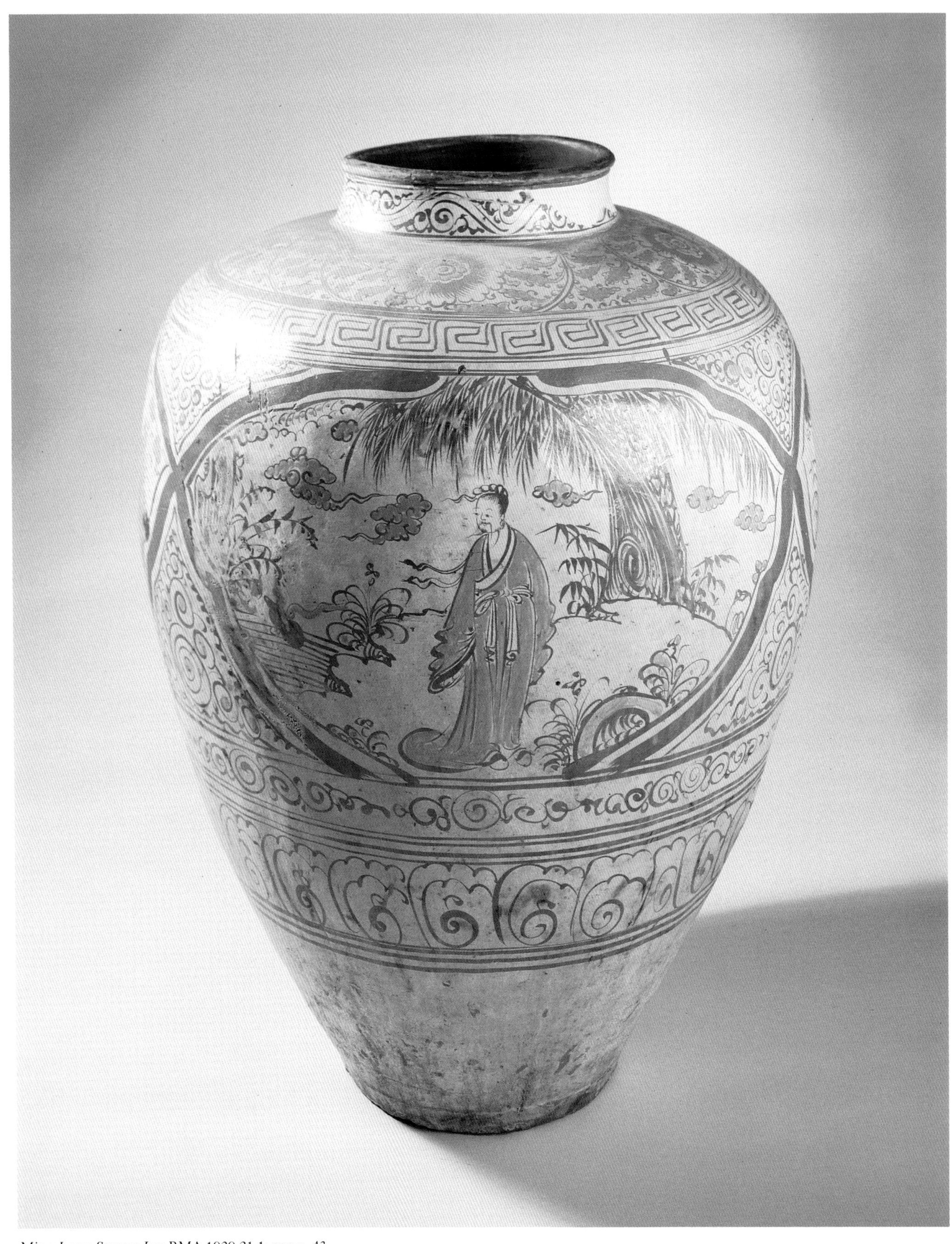

Ming *Large Storage Jar.* BMA 1929.21.1; see p. 43.

FOREWORD

The fine collection of Chinese ceramics at The Baltimore Museum of Art grew through extraordinary generosity on the part of a few prominent members of the Baltimore community, with assistance from a handful of renowned colleagues and dealers. The 400 works in the Asian collection were acquired by gift or purchase over the last sixty-five years. Of these, 100 or so are generally on view in changing installations in the Julius Levy Memorial Gallery which is dedicated to the display of Asian art.

The Baltimore fire of 1904 destroyed most of the city center; in the following years attention was given to improving the city.[1] Central to those civic motivations, The Baltimore Museum of Art was incorporated in November of 1914, even as the First World War had begun the preceding June. On February 22, 1923, the Museum opened to the public at 101 West Monument Street, on Mount Vernon Place, around the corner from Henry Walters's residence and private museum. From the beginning there was an interest in the arts of the Near and Far East. The inaugural exhibition included Near Eastern and Indian metalwork from the collection of Lockwood DeForest, and a year later, Chinese ceramics were shown.[2] In 1929, the Museum moved to its present location on the southern edge of The Johns Hopkins University campus into a building designed by John Russell Pope. One of the first exhibitions in the new facility featured William H. Whitridge's extensive collection of Chinese ceramics.

Among the many individuals actively involved with The Baltimore Museum of Art in those early years, Julius Levy was one of the most prominent.[3] He was a Museum founder in 1914, an original member of the Board of Trustees, and an energetic supporter of the Museum. Mr. Levy's family had lived in Baltimore since the 1870s, and operated a business in men's hats. Straw hats then were extremely popular, and the best straw came from China initially, but from Japan during Mr. Levy's period of activity. His travels to Japan no doubt contributed to his personal interest in the life and culture of the Far East. When Julius Levy died in 1930, a substantial sum of money came to the Museum from his widow Mrs. Etta Levy, and brothers William and Alfred Levy, for the creation of a fund restricted to the purchase of Asian art, as well as a gallery for its display.[4] The Julius Levy Memorial Gallery, designed by Baltimorean John Scarff and constructed with funds from the City of Baltimore, opened on October 13, 1932. With one exception, the works included in the first exhibition were lent by Diedrich Abbes, from the Abbes Collection, and by Ralph Chait Galleries, both of New York City. The Levy Gallery was Baltimore's first and, until The Walters Art Gallery opened to the public in 1934, only space devoted to Asian art, and for nearly a decade, the Levy Fund remained one of only two funds available to the Museum dedicated for the purchase of works of art.

Beginning with the gift from Ralph Chait of a large storage jar (BMA 1929.21.1), the Museum's collection of Asian art grew slowly but steadily, and especially strongly in the area of Chinese ceramics. In 1932, a good collection of Kangxi and later blue-and-white porcelains came by bequest of Baltimorean Francis Burns Harvey. In 1939, the Museum, with the assistance of Edward S. King of The Walters Art Gallery and Theodore S. Hobby of The Metropolitan Museum of Art, was successful in acquiring at auction in New York objects from the William H. Whitridge Collection. The large 1942 bequest of some 1,100 works from the Frank J. and Elizabeth L. Goodnow Collection was followed over the course of the next decade by several smaller gifts, including a number of fine pieces from Lawrason Riggs of J.[5] The Julius Levy Memorial Fund was used again during the 1950s and 1960s for purchases made in consultation with John

Alexander Pope of Washington's distinguished Freer Gallery of Art. At that time also, Cleveland dealer Howard Hollis figured in the growth of the collection, as did local collector Frederick van Slyke. Additional objects from the William H. Whitridge Collection were acquired during the 1970s from Mathilde Whitridge Johnson and William C. Whitridge. The Julius Levy Memorial Gallery was rededicated in 1985, after a complete renovation of the gallery and scholarly evaluation of the collection.[6] At that time, the collection attracted the attention of two important Baltimore collectors, Erwin and Terri Harris, along with prominent Museum colleagues and dealers.[7]

These individuals and many others have enabled The Baltimore Museum of Art to assemble a strong collection devoted almost exclusively to Chinese ceramics. The decision to concentrate on a single aspect of the arts of Asia was determined by the strength and composition of the collection as it evolved over seven decades.[8] This publication documents the most important objects to date in The Baltimore Museum of Art's collection of Chinese ceramics, a collection with a provident past and a promising future.

Frances Klapthor
Associate Curator in Charge
Arts of Asia

NOTES:

1. The history of the Museum has been taken and condensed from Kent Roberts Greenfield, "The Museum: Its First Half Century," *Annual I*, BMA, 1966.
2. Lockwood DeForest provided the ornate, carved Indian paneling as well as furniture which decorated the parlors of 101 West Monument; his connection to Miss M. Carey Thomas, President of Bryn Mawr College and friend of Miss Mary Garrett of Baltimore, no doubt provided the impetus for the purchase (the Museum's first) from Lockwood DeForest's collection of Indian and Near Eastern metalwork.
3. For information on the Levy Family, I am indebted to Mrs. Eleanor Levy and to the remarks prepared for and delivered by Mr. Lester Levy at the Julius Levy Memorial Gallery's 1985 rededication.
4. Although Henry Walters was quite active in the founding of the Museum, being both a member of the City-Wide Congress Committee on Founding an Art Museum and one of its incorporators, his involvement seems not to have extended past that initial phase. In 1931, Baltimore assumed possession of The Walters Art Gallery.
5. Frank Goodnow was the President of The Johns Hopkins University from 1913 until 1929. He was an advisor to Yuan Shi Kai and the first government of the Republic of China, from about 1907 until 1915.

   Unlike other donors, Riggs's connection with Chinese ceramics is not known. His name, however, is worthy of an explanation. There was a custom in Baltimore of adding a man's father's initials to his own name in order to distinguish the son from another member of the family (a cousin or, as in this case, an uncle) bearing the same name. Lawrason Riggs's father's name was Jesse; hence, he became Lawrason Riggs of J. His uncle was Lawrason Riggs.
6. Marianna Shreve Simpson, working with Hin-cheung Lovell, initiated research on the collection in the 1970s. In the 1980s colleagues Louise Cort and Stephen Little consulted with staff and contributed invaluable research and support.
7. Through the Harrises, several dealers became interested in the collection. Guiseppe Eskenazi, Andrew Kahane, and especially James Lally and Sarah Stack have been helpful in bringing objects to the attention of staff, and helping to make their acquisition possible. Colleagues at other institutions have been supportive always, particularly Suzanne Valenstein of The Metropolitan Museum of Art, New York, and Suewhei Hsieh of Towson State University's Asian Art Center. Most recently, New York collectors Peter and Irene Scheinman have been introduced to the collection by Professor Jason Kuo of the University of Maryland, College Park.
8. As well, it should be noted that in adding to the collection by purchase, care has been taken to complement the great strength of Baltimore's Walters Art Gallery in later Chinese porcelains. Thus, the BMA has focused on acquiring stonewares and earthenwares of earlier date.

CATALOGUE OF CHINESE CERAMICS

The present publication catalogues the most notable of the Museum's Chinese ceramics. Thirty-nine works, each illustrated in color, are presented with extended catalogue entries. Another 104 ceramics are cited in abbreviated listing format. In addition to its significant holdings of ceramics, the Museum's Asian collection includes a magnificent gilt bronze life-sized statue of Guanyin, as well as a small number of bronze vessels, gilt bronze images, carved stones, and paintings.

All works are in the collection of The Baltimore Museum of Art (abbreviated throughout as BMA) except for those specifically cited as deriving from the George A. Lucas Collection of The Maryland Institute, College of Art, on extended loan to The Baltimore Museum of Art. The Lucas Collection of Asian art includes altogether about fifty Chinese or Japanese ceramics, all of which have been at the BMA since 1966.

Dimensions are given in inches and centimeters. B.C. dates are also indicated. Provenance (when known) is listed in chronological order, most recent owner first. Chronological order, with the earliest date first, applies to Publication and Exhibition history. References for ceramics included in the abbreviated listings may be obtained from the BMA's Department of the Arts of Asia. Complete bibliographic data appear in the Published/Exhibited section of the entries or under Selected References at the back of the book (short citations appear in Notes).

1

Western Han period
(206 B.C.–A.D. 8)

FIGURE OF A STANDING HORSE

(c. 2nd century B.C.)
Red earthenware with red slip and traces of pigment, encrustation
23 5/8 in. long (60 cm.)
Julius Levy Memorial Fund
BMA 1987.1a-b

Published/Exhibited: J. J. Lally & Co., New York, December 3–17, 1986, lot 18; Donna K. Strahan and Ann Boulton, "Chinese Ceramic Quadrupeds: Construction and Restoration," *The Conservation of Far Eastern Art* (Preprints of the Contributions to the Kyoto Congress, September 19–23, 1988), London, The International Institute of Historic and Artistic Works, 1988, pp. 150–152, ill. figs. 3, 4, 9, and 11.

This horse epitomizes the iconic quality inherent in the best mortuary sculpture of the Han dynasty. The energy and power it conveys are also characteristic. Tension results from its dual qualities of implied and arrested motion. The horse was mold-made of red earthenware; nine molds were probably required which, it is conjectured, were prepared for use by coating with a parting compound to prevent the clay from sticking, and assembled prior to firing.[1] Two impressions of assembly or firing supports remain just in front of the rear legs. After being covered with slip, a watery clay coating, and painted with vivid pigments, the horse was provided with a bridle and probably more extensive trappings as well.

By the first century B.C. the Chinese had a tradition of burying goods with their dead that extended back at least to the fifth millennium. The observance of this tradition evolved over time. At its grandest scale, during the late Shang (c. 13th–11th century B.C.), enormous pit tombs were constructed which contained such status goods as elaborate bronze vessels, carved jade ornaments, silk and foodstuffs, as well as both animal and human sacrificial victims.[2] Not infrequently, horses and chariots or carriages were buried in subsidiary pits; real carriages and horses were still used in some tombs of the nobility in the middle Western Han but were replaced by wood and clay replicas by the end of the period.[3] The most immediate precedent for this and similar figures was the tomb complex of Qin Shihuangdi which was found to contain an army of at least 7,000 larger-than-life-sized soldiers and horses.

In fact, the Han dynasty was founded on rebellion against the harsh rule of Qin; once the First Emperor died, his successors were unable to quell dissent. After a period of civil war, the Han dynasty (206 B.C.–A.D. 220) was established by the former head of a posting station, a native of Jiangsu province. Warfare was nearly continuous throughout the Western Han period. From 206 to 130 B.C., the army consisted of an enormous body of infantrymen who surrounded chariots and were supported by cavalry.[4] This formation, based on the Qin model, was ill suited for battle with the Xiongnu, mounted nomads with larger and stronger steeds, who encroached along the northern border.

During the second century the emperor Wu Di (140–87 B.C.) attempted to enlist allies against the Xiongnu. In 138 he sent an ambassador to find the Yuezhi, a tribe that had been driven from Gansu province by the Xiongnu and had relocated in Afghanistan. On his way, Zhang Qian went to Dayuan, known in the west as Ferghana or Sogdiana, one of the easternmost provinces of Alexander the Great's empire. There he found "superb horses which sweat blood."[5] After Wu Di's death, China succeeded in taking control of Dayuan in Ferghana, thereby establishing contact with Western Asia. The Chinese exported silk, the production of which was their secret and monopoly, and in return obtained horses and other goods.

Horses were essential in both establishing and exerting control during the Western Han. The Baltimore Museum's horse resembles those discovered at Yangjiawan, Xianyang, Shaanxi (c. 179–141 B.C.), although the latter are constructed of gray earthenware. A red clay horse, with a similar profile, was discovered in Jiangsu province at Xiaoshanzi, Guishan (suburbs of Xuzhou) in 1958.[6]

1. It is likely that dry powdered clay was used; see Strahan and Boulton, 1988, p. 150.
2. The sites referred to, including especially Xiaocun and Xibeigang, are located in northern Henan province; see Chang, pp. 317–339. As Robert Thorp noted in the exhibition catalogue, *The Great Bronze Age of China: An Exhibition from The People's Republic of China* (New York: The Metropolitan Museum of Art and Alfred A. Knopf, Inc., 1980), "Human sacrifice was pervasive at the late Shang sites...oracle bones make it clear that the ancestors derived their strength in part from offerings of wine, flesh, and blood," p. 56.
3. Wang Zhongshu, p. 208.
4. Pirazzoli-t'Serstevens, p. 28.
5. Fitzgerald, p. 227.
6. Professor Robert Thorp of Washington University brought this comparable object to my attention.

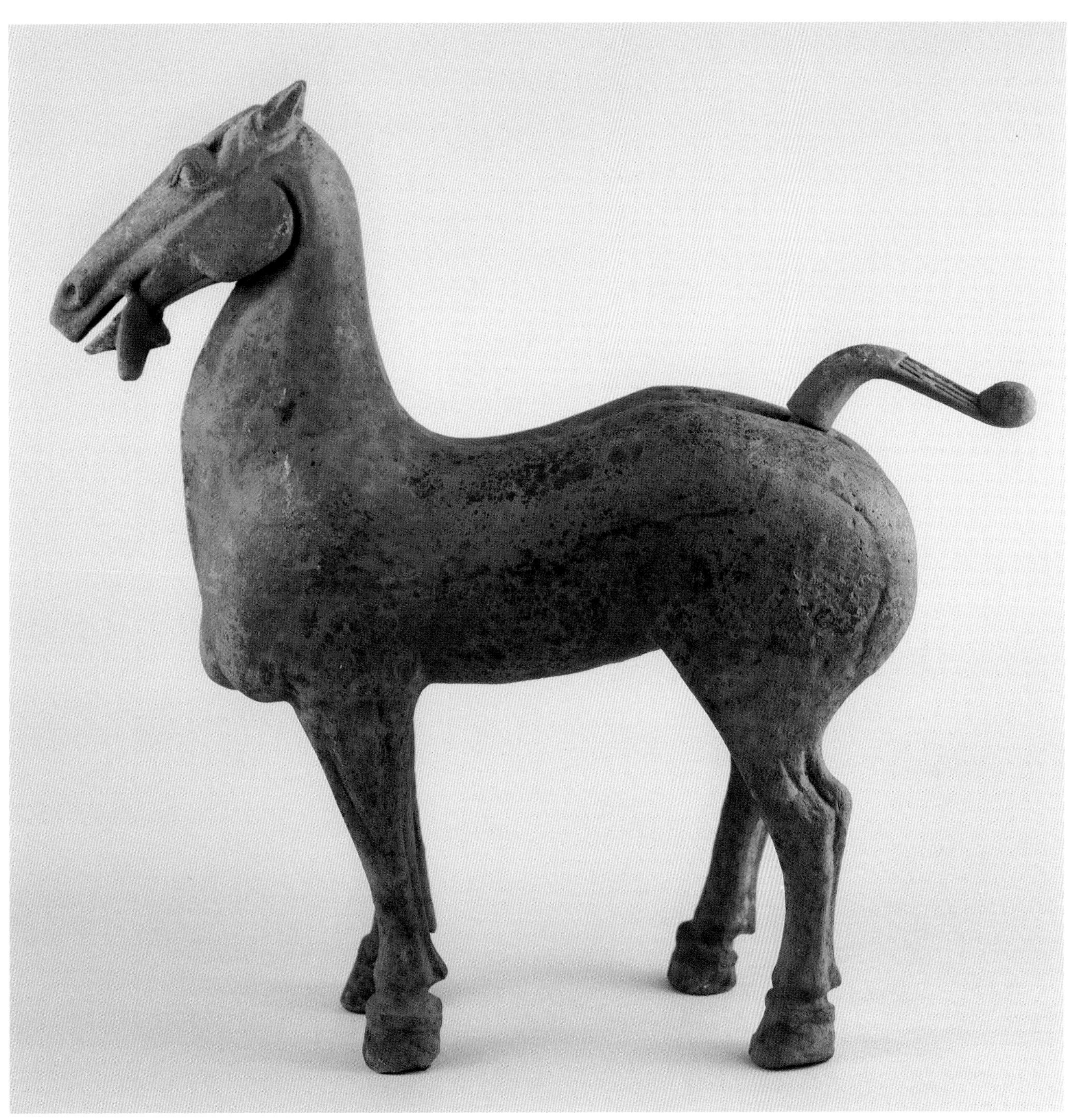

2

Han dynasty (206 B.C.–A.D. 220)

WINE STORAGE VESSEL (HU)

Red earthenware with amber lead-fluxed glaze
19 1/2 in. high (49.5 cm.)
Gift of J. J. Lally & Co., New York
BMA 1991.118

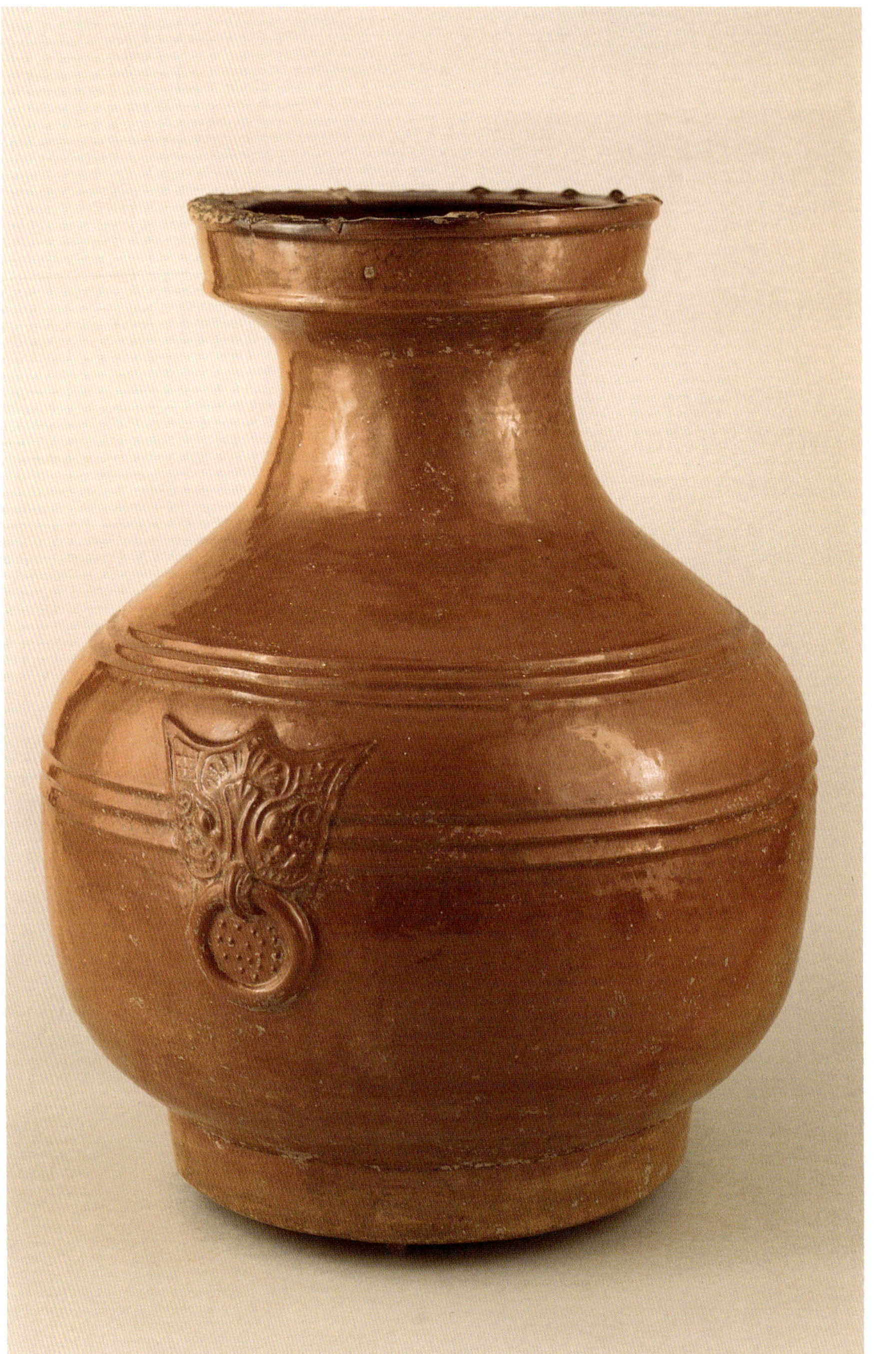

While the Chinese belief in the afterlife was ancient, extending back into prehistory, the perception of it evolved over the ensuing millennia, and its coeval, the shaft tomb, evolved as well. What had been conceived of as a treasure chest in the 16th–6th centuries B.C., containing objects of great intrinsic value, became by the 1st–2nd centuries A.D. a model dwelling, a multichambered abode filled with less-costly objects made specifically for burial. Bronzes and jades came to be replaced by lacquer, pottery, and silk, though the number of lacquerwares decreased during the Eastern Han.[1]

The most remarkable feature of this exceptionally large vessel is its rich, bright color that was obtained by the addition of small amounts of iron oxide and lead oxide to the glaze. The added iron imparted the even amber color, while the lead reduced the temperature at which the glaze melted and secondarily produced the glassiness that in this case is quite mesmerizing. Lead-glazed earthenwares can be documented as early as the late 2nd–early 1st century B.C.; during the Han dynasty, they typically were fired once after the application of the glaze.[2] The vessel was mold-made of red earthenware, decorated with applied monster-mask handles and rouletted triangle-bands on its broad shoulder, glazed, and fired upside down. The monster-masks (*taotie*) are themselves of ancient origin, found embellishing ritual bronzes from the 11th century B.C. on.

1. Wang Zhongshu, p. 207.
2. Valenstein, p. 45, and also p. 47, where she notes that lead-glazed wares reportedly "have been found in the vicinity of Xian, Shaanxi province in a tomb that is datable to the Wudi period, 141–87 B.C."

3

Eastern Han period (25–220)

TRIPOD VESSEL WITH ACROBATS BALANCED ON THE RIM

(c. 200)
Earthenware with pink, red, orange, and black pigments applied over white slip
7 5/8 in. high (19.4 cm.)
Julius Levy Memorial Fund
BMA 1988.2

Provenance: Andrew Kahane, Limited, New York

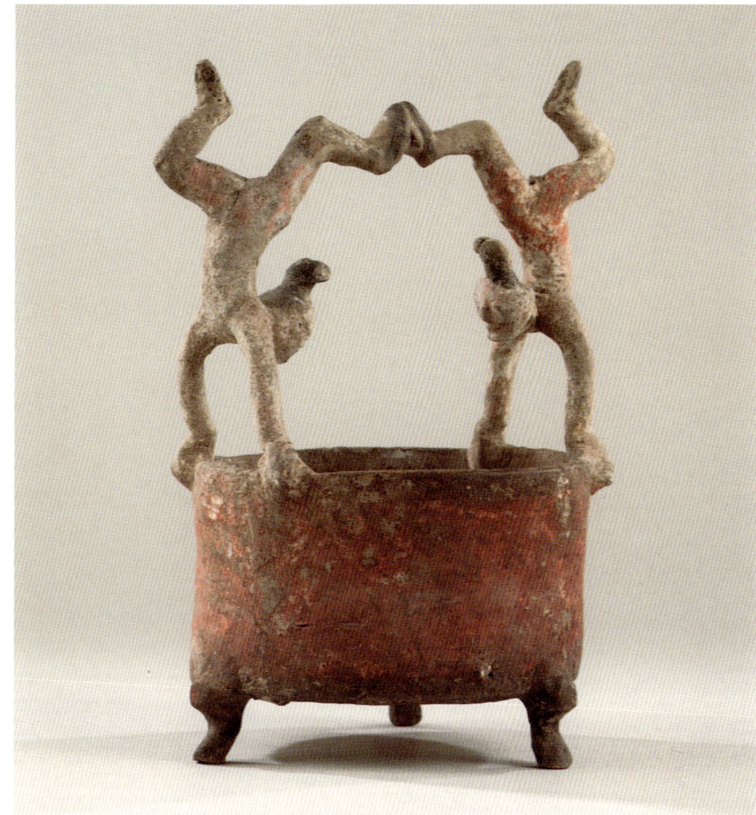

Whereas the Western Han period was dominated by ever-present warfare conducted for expansion as well as defense, domestic concerns were primary during the Eastern Han. The period began and ended with civil war. In the intervening two centuries, large and powerful estates appeared especially in the central plain; these became essentially self-sufficient by combining agriculture with industry, at the expense of small landowners. Not surprisingly, the mortuary pottery of the Eastern Han period reflects these preoccupations. Figures of farm animals and buildings are numerous; tiles that decorate the walls of Sichuan tombs overwhelmingly portray agricultural or industrial activities. Another element of life preserved in the grave goods was more lighthearted: figures of dancers, acrobats, jugglers, and musicians are prominent, as again are scenes of many types of entertainment on the tomb tiles of Sichuan province. These figures are often surprisingly successful at capturing an expression, a gesture, a moment's grace and exuberance, but on a scale much reduced from that of the marvelous Western Han horse (BMA 1987.1).

This charming object portrays two young girls, who are perhaps more contortionists than acrobats, as they balance on their hands on the rim of a wine-warming vessel (*wenjiucun*), bent backwards, with legs meeting over the center of the tripod.[1] There is the further possibility that they may represent immortals who inhabited the court of the Queen Mother of the West (*Xiwangmu*), in a perpetual state of diversions and delights.[2] Popular Daoism and the associated cult of immortality spread widely during the 2nd century, and images of the deities and inhabitants of the afterlife were included in the tombs of this period.

Two other like objects are in the collection of the Musée Cernuschi, Paris,[3] and another with three figures was discovered in 1972 near Luoyang in Henan province from an Eastern Han tomb.[4]

1. The double-knot hairstyle worn by the figures identifies them as females; see Kenneth J. DeWoskin, "Music and Entertainment Themes in Han Funerary Sculpture," *Orientations* 18, no. 4 (April 1987): 35.
2. The bronze and clay "money trees" unique to Sichuan province show acrobats flanking Xiwangmu above Kunlun, the paradisiacal mountain home of the immortals; see Wu Hung, "Xiwangmu, the Queen Mother of the West," *Orientations* 18, no. 4 (April 1987): 30–31, and Lim, p. 160.
3. They were published in *Art d'Extrême Orient* (Paris: Jacques Barrère Art d'extrême Orient, 1987), p. 18, no. 47, and in *Arts and Asiatiques* 44 (1989): 120, fig. 3.
4. Published in *Kaogu*, 1975, vol. 2, pp. 116–123, 134.

4

Eastern Han period (25–220)

TOWER SURROUNDED BY A MOAT

(2nd century)
Earthenware with green lead-fluxed glaze
Tower: 21 5/8 in. high (55 cm.);
basin: 16 3/8 in. diam. (41.5 cm.)
Julius Levy Memorial Fund,
by exchange
BMA 1988.640

Published/Exhibited: Christie's, New York, December 1, 1988, sale 6720, lot 169, pp. 88–89.

The tower, composed of a tiled roof and single platform, is raised on stilts from a moat in the form of a basin. There are nine figures in the tower, and various animals (foxes, dogs, or rabbits) and birds (geese) on the rim of the basin, and reptiles (frogs, turtle), birds (geese, ducks, crane), and fish in the interior. The floor of the platform has a round opening in the center; astride the hole is a dancer.[1] Facing the dancer are four kneeling figures, their hands raised and apart as if clapping.[2] Standing at each corner of the balcony, facing outward, is an archer with drawn crossbow. Four birds are seated on the ridged, tiled roof at each corner, with an additional two seated on the peak.

Chinese religion since ancient times was bound inextricably with the natural world, and the position of man within it; the five directions and features of geography, such as mountains, rivers, woods, as well as birds and animals, were the means by which man's alignment was determined.[3] "The state provided for shrines to be built to honor the lords of the rain or the winds, or the guardian spirits of certain holy rivers or mountains. Each locality in the empire was commanded to conduct its own worship and sacrifices to the local protecting spirits."[4] Towers, which derived significance from their association with mountains, were included among Han religious structures and were used to communicate with the world of the immortals.

Another ritual structure, the spirit terrace, was used to observe the auspicious Heavenly signs which inevitably ensued upon the proper completion of imperial rites.[5] "The Book of Songs occasionally refers to birds alighting on the roof as symbols of Heavenly favor and this image maintained its meaning in Han times...their presence on a roof was indicative of the gathering of spirits...abundant fish in a moat are also listed among the blessings and auspicious signs depicted on a stone from Shandong dated either 424 or 151 AD."[6]

While it is impossible to determine the precise nature of this tower, some ritual function is strongly suggested by the presence of the birds and the fish, as well as by the performance being given.

1. The corresponding figure on a similar structure has been identified as the owner of the tomb. See George Kuwayama, "The Sculptural Development of Ceramic Funerary Figures in China," in *The Quest for Eternity* (Los Angeles: Los Angeles County Museum of Art, Chronicle Books, 1987), p. 114, no. 29.
2. This position is typically assumed by the figures of Liubo players, which also were included in burial retinues of the time; the flat-topped hats worn by three of the four are like those worn by Liubo players. Liubo was a board game, the rules of which are unknown, but a link has been made between the game board used for it and the cosmological features which decorate some mirror backs.
3. The five directions are the four cardinal directions plus center.
4. Michael Loewe, *Everyday Life in Early Imperial China During the Han Period 202 B.C.–A.D. 220* (New York: Dorset Press, 1968), p. 109.
5. Powers, p. 236.
6. Powers, p. 234.

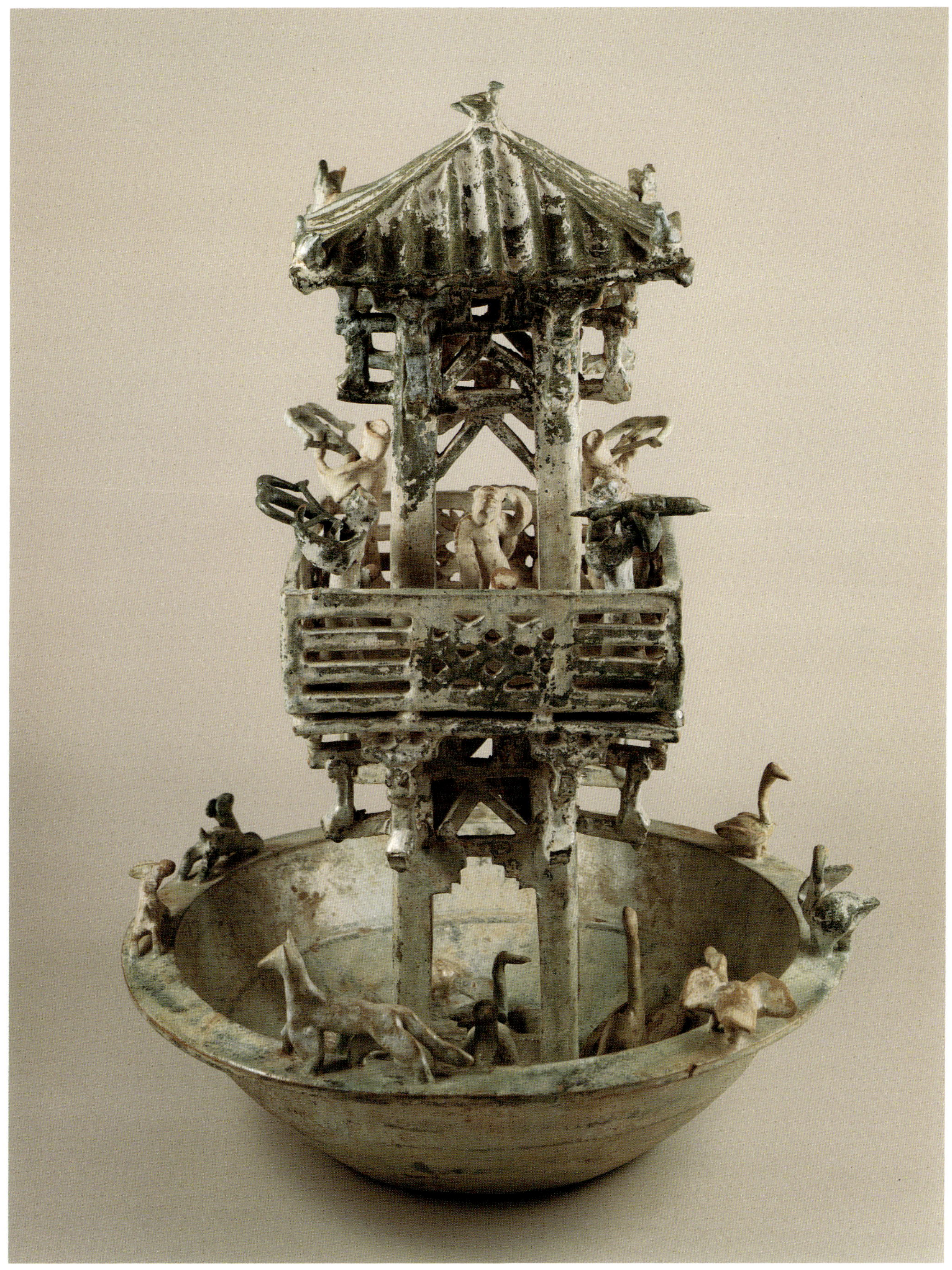

5

Zhejiang province
Han dynasty (206 B.C.–A.D. 220)

STORAGE VESSEL (GUAN)

Stoneware with remnants of greenish-brown glaze
14 in. diam. (35.5 cm.)
Julius Levy Memorial Fund
BMA 1992.23

Provenance: Anthony R. Derham, New York

Published/Exhibited: Christie's, New York, November 27, 1991, sale 7366, lot 254, ill.

By the end of the Warring States period (475–221 B.C.) and throughout the Han dynasty, an area in northern Zhejiang province along the coast as well as southern Jiangsu province was routinely producing glazed stoneware vessels. Many derived from bronze *guan* or *hu* prototypes. These storage jars were typically decorated with an overall stamped pattern, or with a combination of incised lines and raised bands, and glazed only on their upper surfaces. It has been suggested that dry wood-ash or a mixture of dry clay and ash was sifted over the damp pots before firing.[1]

This jar is distinguished by an exceptionally dynamic profile as well as a crisply stamped repeating small comb pattern.[2] Well suited to pottery and used since neolithic times, overall surface texture often decorated utilitarian vessels. Textiles, cords, coins, and dies were used variously to produce the decoration.

The dark gray stoneware body oxidized to a brick red in certain areas, and remnants of high-lime glaze remain on the shoulder.[3] This early stoneware evolved into the Yue ware of the 3rd–6th century centered in the same region, and ultimately into the great Longquan celadons of southern Zhejiang province.

1. *Iron in the Fire*, p. 31.
2. Comb-decorated fragments have been found at Shangyu, a major center for greenwares, and Ningbo, both located in northern Zhejiang; see nos. 1 and 26 in Hughes-Stanton and Kerr, for comparable fragments. Kilns at Shaoxing, another important center in the same vicinity, produced similar jars as well.
3. The earliest stoneware glazes were of this type; its characteristic color is greenish-yellow or olive due to iron and titanium. Because of their tendency to run, these glazes were applied thinly; often they exhibit a frosted dullness. See *Iron in the Fire*, p. 12.

6

Zhejiang province
Western Jin dynasty (265–316)

SOUL URN (HUN PING)

Stoneware with olive green glaze
17 1/4 in. high (43.5 cm.)
Frank J. and Elizabeth L. Goodnow Collection, by exchange
BMA 1988.647

Provenance: J. J. Lally & Co., New York; Stanley and Adele Herzman, New York

Published/Exhibited: Sotheby's, New York, December 4, 1985, lot 85, pp. 84–85; J. J. Lally & Co., New York, May 27–June 18, 1988, lot 47.

Vessels of this type represent another variation of the mountain abode of the immortals. While a large number of these jars have been discovered in the last thirty years, this particular example incorporates interesting iconography and at the same time illustrates a particularly successful glazed stoneware identified as early celadon.

Raised above the elongated ovoid body on top of the shoulder is a two-tiered superstructure. The lower level is round; on it, there are two covered gates with inverted dragon-head columns and four pillars (*que*) which support the upper level. Between the gates on either side of the urn there are five molded figures of the Buddha seated on lotus plinths and one Daoist kneeling. On the upper square level there are four large round jars at each corner and between them two Daoists kneeling in front of four openings. A double-hipped, ridged roof surmounted by a crescent finial hangs over the upper level. There is no detachable lid.

As early as the Shang dynasty, the Chinese had conceived of two-part soul, composed of the *hun* and the *po*. The *hun* was the sentient emanation of the *yang* principle—the embodiment of masculine attributes such as light, heat, intelligence—which upon death left the body in order to dwell on a higher plane inhabited by the immortals and ancestors. The more material and animating *po*—the feminine, dark, cold, physical *yin* element—remained with the body. That there could be some continuing interaction between the two is suggested by the survivors' entreaties to the *hun* as contained in The Great Summons (3rd–2nd century B.C.), "...O Soul, come back to idleness and peace...O Soul, come back to joys beyond all telling...come back to feed on foods you love...come back and bring prosperity to house and stock!"[1] An early view of these urns postulated that they were used in the absence of a body, as a substitute for the lingering or returning soul.[2]

The combined presence of Buddhas and Daoists is somewhat unusual and must reflect the accelerated expansion of Buddhism in the century following the collapse of the Han dynasty. The inclusion of the pillar gates, a common feature on these urns, is noteworthy. These gates during the Han dynasty were the prerogative of high-ranking officials, and were used in the construction of palaces, city gates, entrance doors, and tombs. More significantly, "the *que* pillar gate in Sichuan art always symbolizes the passage of the soul of the deceased into the spiritual world."[3]

Early in the development of their ceramic history, the Chinese gained proficiency with clays fired to high temperatures (1100 to 1280 degrees Celsius), resulting in an impermeable and extremely durable ceramic known as stoneware. The high firing temperatures limited the glazes to more somber colors, primarily browns and greens.[4] By the end of the 3rd century, gray stoneware bodies were routinely covered with green glaze, in a tremendous range of quality. This example is distinguished by its fine, dense body and clear, even, olive glaze.

Compared to others of its type, this vessel is sparsely arrayed with figures and jars. It is, however, this simplicity combined with the quality of the materials that give the object its strong visual impact.

1. Arthur Waley, trans., *Chinese Poems* (1982; reprint, London: Unwin Paperbacks, 1989), pp. 32–37.
2. Wai-kam Ho, "Hun-p'ing Urn of the Soul," *Cleveland Museum of Art Bulletin* 28 (February 1961): 26–34.
3. Lim, p. 107.
4. Browns result from an oxygen-rich atmosphere within the kiln, while a smoky, oxygen-poor atmosphere that steals oxygen molecules from the fired clay vessels produces a wide range of blacks, grays, and greens.

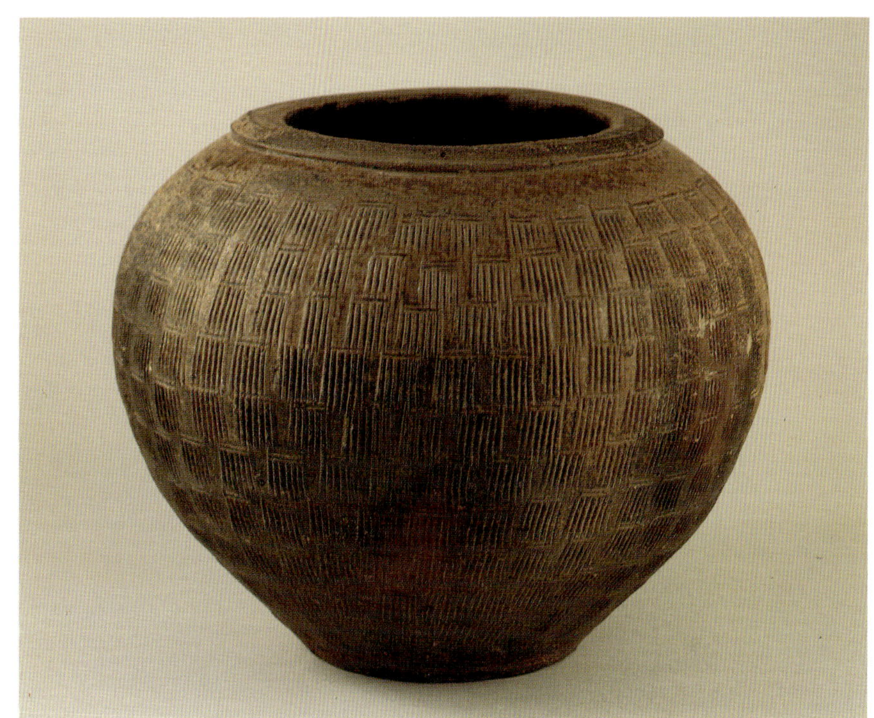

5

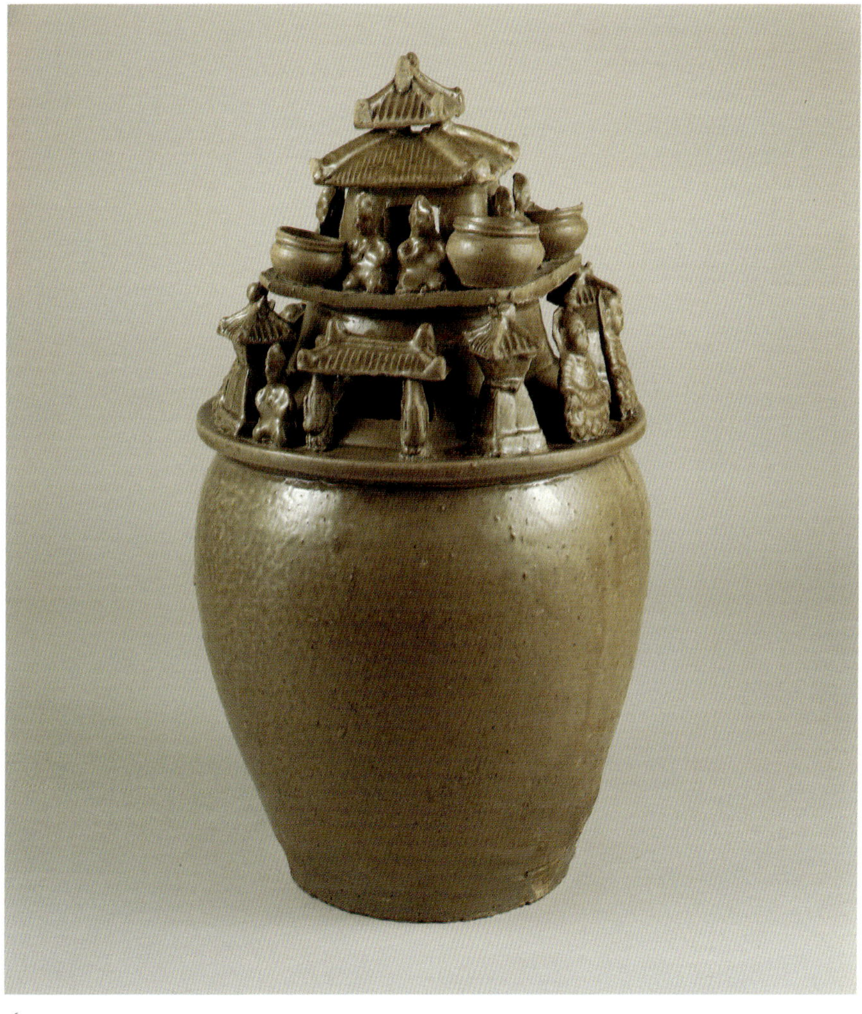

6

7

Tang dynasty (618–907)

PAIR OF CAMELS WITH FOREIGN RIDERS

(7th century)
Earthenware with traces of pigment and burial encrustation
.1) 15 in. long (38 cm.); .2) 16 in. long (42 cm.)
Julius Levy Memorial Fund
BMA 1950.65.1-2

Provenance: C. K. Chang, Baltimore

Published/Exhibited: *The Morning Sun*, Baltimore, July 26, 1950.

This pair of irascible camels ridden by two haughty foreigners illustrates the exuberant realism characteristic of the best mortuary pottery produced during the first half of the Tang dynasty. Moreover, it permits the consideration of the important position occupied by foreign goods and peoples in China at that time.

The spirit articles (*mingqi*) of the Western Han and Six Dynasties portray soldiers and horses prepared for battle, reflecting the military concerns of the periods. Mortuary pottery of the Eastern Han period suggests the predominance of agrarian activities at that time. Similarly, many such objects produced during the Tang dynasty attest to the significance of trade then. Peoples from across western and central Asia, as well as from east Asia, were drawn to the Tang dynasty metropolis of Changan; this capital was likely the largest, most important city in the world during the 7th and early 8th centuries.[1] A sizeable portion of its inhabitants were foreigners. Some were missionaries, others were entertainers and performers of various types, many no doubt were adventure-seekers, some were slaves; most were involved with trade.[2] While the southern sea routes were no less important, Changan was located on the north-central plain; thus its trade was dominated by the great roads leading to the west. There were two ways overland, a northern and a southern route, both equally dangerous; camels provided the main means of transport.[3] The men associated with the camels were from Central Asia. Although identification of these particular Central Asians remains elusive, it is probable that they were Sogdians.[4]

The riders wear soft felt hats and heavy jackets that retain traces of ornate brocade designs which derive from Persian motifs. The positioning of their upper bodies is the same as for freestanding glazed and unglazed grooms, indicating that the figures were mold-made with substantial modeling.

1. Schafer gives a mid-8th-century population for Changan of almost two million inhabitants. Constantinople had a population of some one million in the 6th century while Baghdad had in the 9th century possibly two million inhabitants.
2. The peoples represented in Changan in the late 7th–early 8th century included Arabs, Persians, and Indians, and the religions practiced there included those from the West, Judaism, Christianity (Manichaeism), and Islam, in addition to Buddhism and Daoism.
3. The northern route led through Turfan, Kucha, and Samarkand; the southern through Khotan and Kashgar. Both terminated at Antioch on the coast of Syria.
4. Watson notes that "the features are strongly modelled, with the large nose thought to be a characteristic of all western peoples, although it is most likely to have been a peculiarity of Sogdian merchants," p. 183. Ezekiel Schloss in *Foreigners in Ancient Chinese Art* (New York: China House Gallery, China Institute in America, 1969), on the other hand, identifies foreigners more precisely but less consistently; those that resemble these men are variously Caucaso-Iranians, Uigher Turks, Semitic Armenoids, or generic West Asians (cat. nos. 3, 6, 9, 10, 16, 43). Sogdians identified by him are clean-shaven.

8

Tang dynasty (618–907)

FIGURE OF A COURT LADY

(first half of the 8th century)
Earthenware with traces of orange and black pigments over white slip
15 7/8 in. high (40.3 cm.)
Julius Levy Memorial Fund
BMA 1986.76

Published/Exhibited: Sotheby's, New York, June 3, 1986, sale 5469, lot 167.

Not only foreigners but also Chinese ladies, officials, dignitaries, attendants, and the like were portrayed in the mortuary pottery of north China. The figures of the ladies are interesting for the information they provide on fashion and ideas of beauty during the first half of the Tang dynasty.

Before the late 7th century, ladies were all of slender proportion, elegant but girlish. By the beginning of the 8th century, a different profile predominates. These ladies are fleshy and alluring; their robes fall in deep folds and their hair is worn in a variety of fanciful styles which had such poetic names as "falling off a horse" style (*duomaji*), or "thicket" or "overgrown" style (*congji*).[1] This particular style has been identified as the "side butterfly bun."[2] The figures have traditionally been identified with Yang Guifei, the concubine of Emperor Xuanzong (713–756). In fact, the presence of these ladies in tombs, such as the tomb of General Xianyu Tinglui who died in 723, predates her ascendancy at court.[3]

1. *Tang*, pp. 56–59, nos. 28–29.
2. Ezekiel Schloss, *Ancient Chinese Ceramic Sculpture from Han through T'ang* (Stamford, Connecticut: Castle Publishing Company, 1977), p. 153, no. 67.
3. *Tang*, p. 56, no. 28.

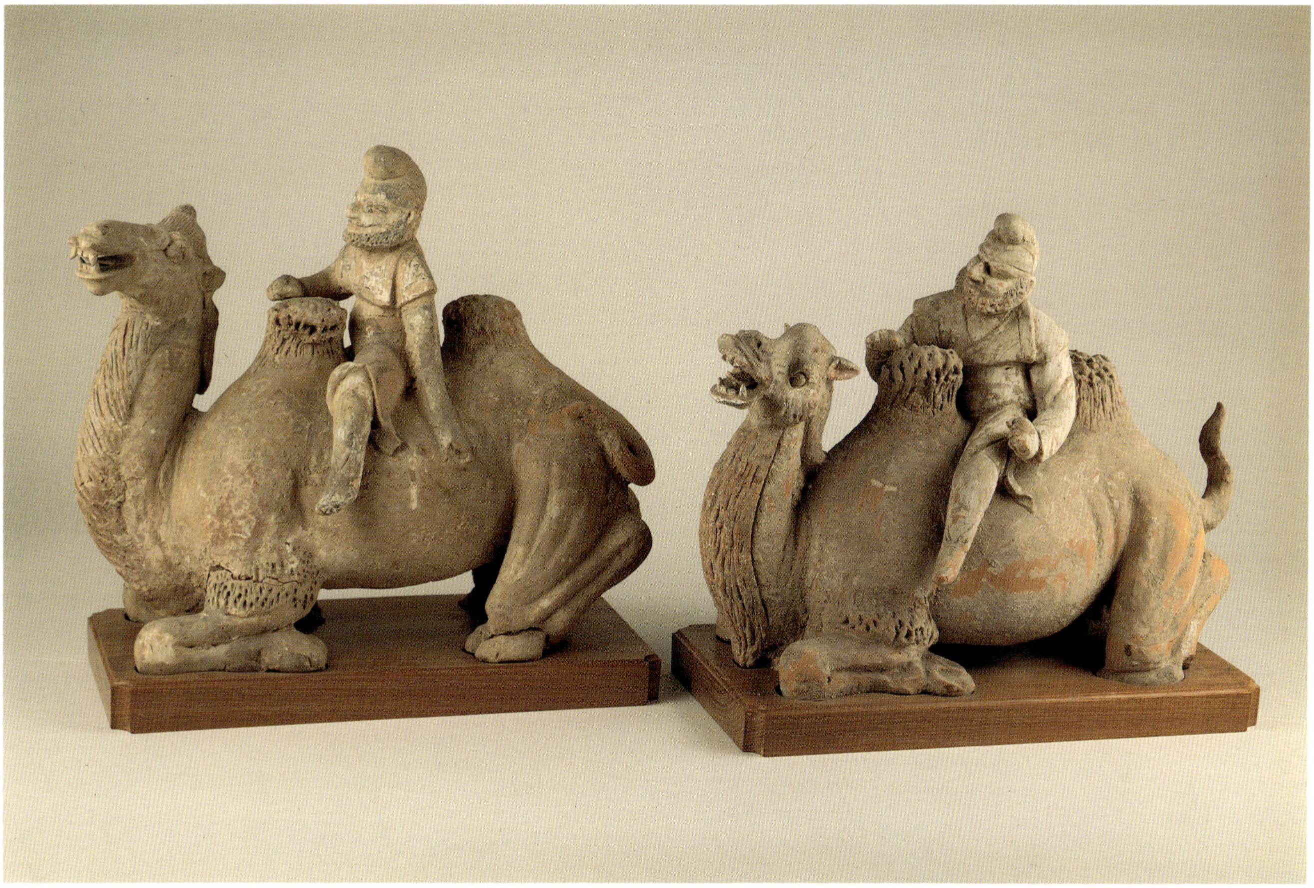

7

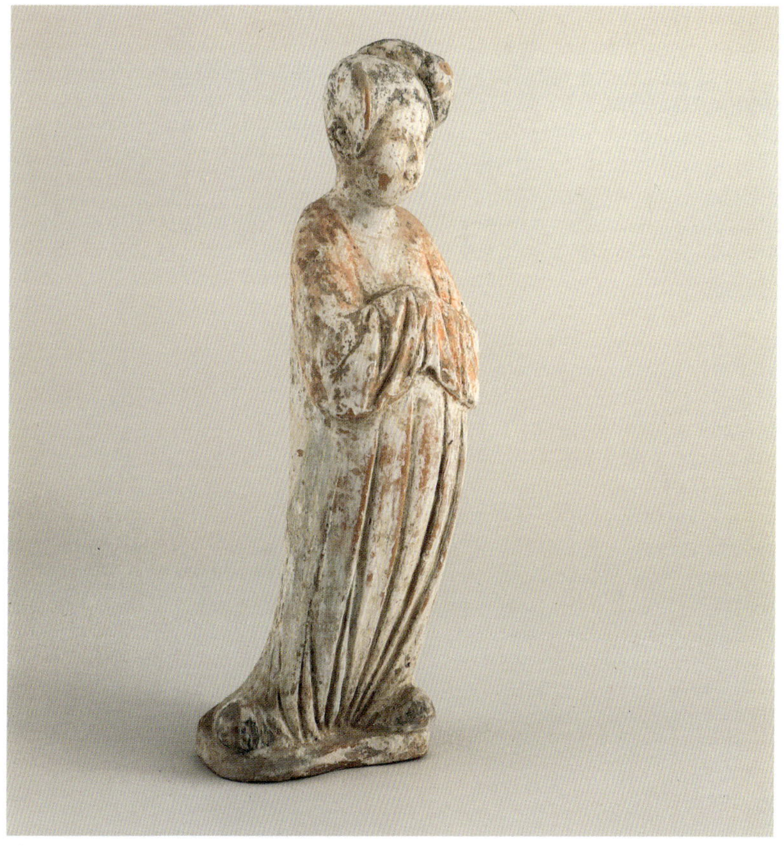

8

9

Possibly Shaanxi province
Tang dynasty (618–907)

PAIR OF TOMB GUARDIANS

(c. 725–750)
White earthenware with orange, pink, black, green, and red pigments
.1) lion: 28 in. high (71.4 cm.);
.2) man: 28 13/16 in. high (73.2 cm.)
Purchase with exchange funds from Bequest of John M. Glenn, Gift of Alexander B. Griswold, Gift of Mr. and Mrs. L. Manuel Hendler, The Mary Frick Jacobs Collection, Gift of Randolph Mordecai, Gift from the Estate of Ruth Marshall Mugford, and Gift of Elizabeth Remsen; and Julius Levy Memorial Fund
BMA 1991.119.1-2

Provenance: J. J. Lally & Co., New York

These spectacular guardian figures represent the apex of mortuary pottery. Ancient beings associated with burial, the pair commands attention as ambitious clay sculpture, and as evidence of the kind of extensive, vivid polychrome decoration that has seldom survived intact. Their size, complex construction, and colorful decoration including the use of gold leaf indicate that they were entombed with an important member of the Tang elite. Unlike the figures of horses, camels, or various attendants, scores of which were placed in tombs, only two of these paired guardians would have been needed. The figures have been found facing each other in the tomb path that leads to the coffin chamber, a position which corresponds to the Han dynasty (206 B.C.–220 A.D.) placement at the tomb entrance.[1]

The two creatures are descended from guardian figures of a pre-Han tradition. A number of beings, malevolent as well as protective, were manifest in those beliefs; some threatened the deceased's soul or survivors, others protected both. Being the place where the worlds of the living and the dead met, the tomb occupied a critical if precarious position; therefore, guardian figures were necessary. Among the earliest of these figures, interred in Warring States period (475–221 B.C.) tombs from the southerly state of Chu, were lacquered wood creatures. They were commonly portrayed with two antlers and exceedingly long tongues, and sometimes round bulging eyes as well, attributes still employed a thousand years later for protecting Tang dynasty tombs.

During the Han dynasty (206 B.C.–A.D. 220), important tombs began to be equipped with a Spirit Road, an avenue lined by large stone sculptures leading to the entrance of the tomb. The earliest known group of such sculptures dates from the 2nd century B.C., and includes tigers, horses, oxen, elephants, and fish. The evolution of apotropaic beings is evident in Spirit Road sculpture. Most extant Eastern Han sculptures were based on the tiger, in many guises, sometimes with wings or other supernatural attributes.[2] The tiger was well-known in the Han as the animal emblem of the west and as king of the wild, the symbol of courage, dignity, and military prowess; above all a guardian against evil spirits, it was able to summon the wind, a vital means of communicating with the spirit world.[3] The addition of wings, horns, and beards to the large felines seems to have been simply a question of style, although the more fanciful forms were favored in Shaanxi and Henan, perhaps inspired by Warring States bronze talismans; sometimes the name was carved on the flank or shoulder, the most popular among the names being *tianlu*, *bixie*, and *qilin*.[4] Meng Kang's Wei Kingdom (220–265) annotation of the Han History (Han Shu) includes the following description of the *bixie* (one who averts evil) and *tianlu* (heavenly deer): "If it has one horn, it may be a tianlu; if it has two horns, it may be a bixie."[5] In addition to these (horns, long tongues, large eyes, wings, and beards), a human face, serpentine body, serrated spine, and hooved feet are among the recurrent features of composite, apotropaic creatures, from the Eastern Han on; moreover, these creatures have been found in either a striding or a crouched position. By the early 6th century, the lion was adopted as the basis for one guardian frequently paired with a grotesque, human-faced counterpart. The special efficacy of a pair—one to hear heavenly messages, the other to avert evil—has been noted.[6]

While the lion initially appeared as an alter ego of the tiger, by the Tang dynasty it assumed ascendancy over the tiger, its spiritual potency exaggerated beyond that of the traditional tiger.[7] When the emperor Taizong received in 635 a tribute lion, he ordered a commemorative rhapsody:

> *It glares its eyes—and lightning flashes,*
> *It vents its voice—and thunder echoes.*
> *It drags away the tiger,*
> *Swallows down the bear,*
> *Splits the rhinoceros,*
> *Cleaves the elephant...*

Even body parts of the beast were imbued with power. "Flies and gnats did not dare to light on a duster made from a lion's tail...if a musician strummed a zither strung with lion sinews, all other strings in the orchestra would break, this idea apparently being related to the lion's terrifying scream." The majestic animal, furthermore, was closely associated with Buddhism. Its roar was known to be the voice of the Buddha, himself a lion among men, teaching his laws; wherever the Buddha sat was known as the "seat of the lion," thus the use of the lion throne both for the Buddha and his monks.

While the evolution of the iconography may be especially compelling, aspects of the construction and decoration are no less significant. The use of the higher-firing white earthenware resulted in fully sculptural clay figures, suitable not only for the bright lead-fluxed glazes common to mortuary pottery but also for the painter's palette of unfired mineral pigments. These were

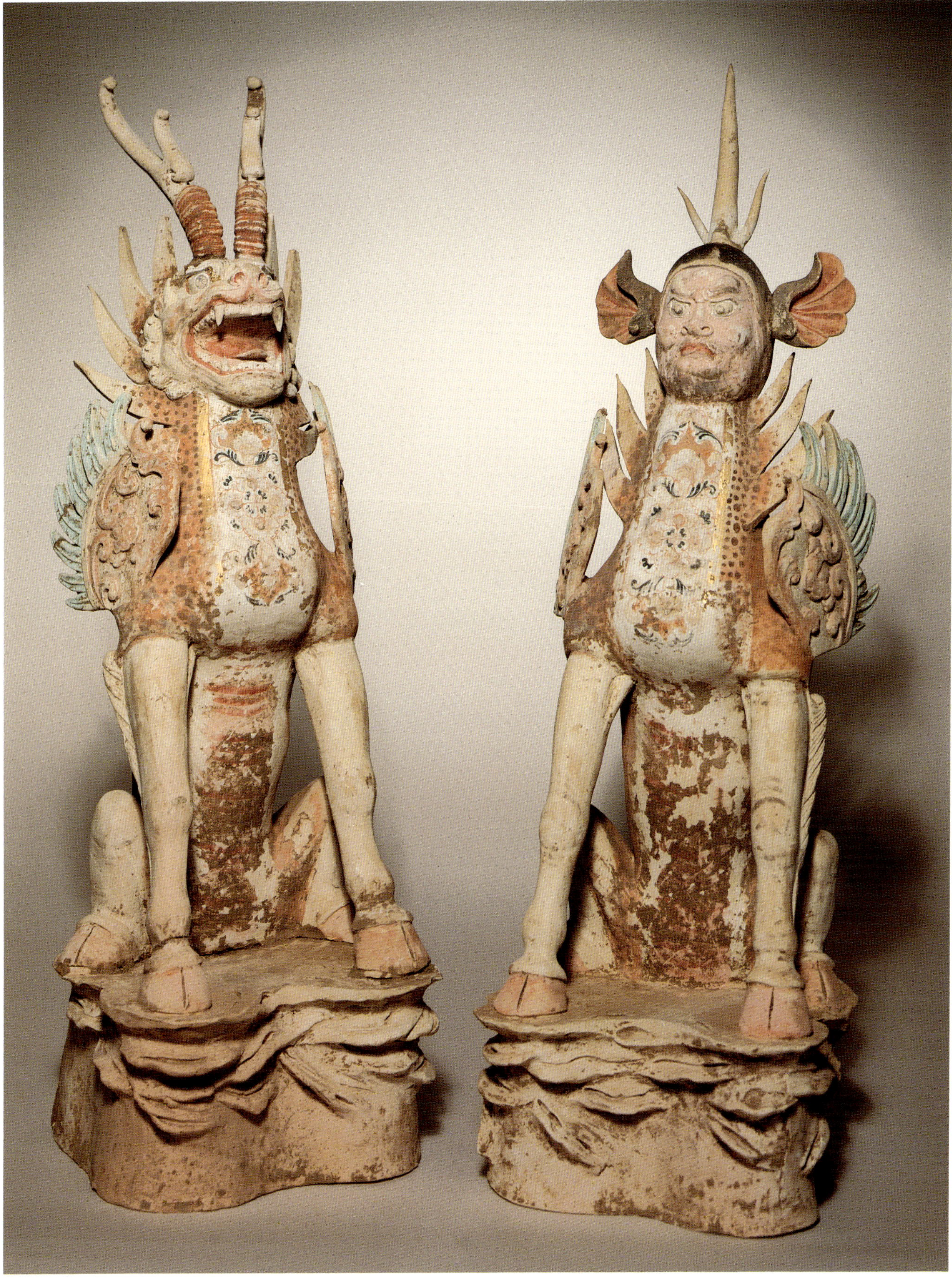

used here to depict an elaborate, brocade-like floral medallion on the upper chest, and an overall spotted pattern on the back of each figure, as well as certain delicate facial features such as the beard. Less common on pottery figures than the painted decoration is the raised ornament found on the wings which recalls the kind of carved stone decoration prevalent at the time.[8] The careful, expert execution of these particular guardian figures animates their ancient and complex meaning.

1. Mary H. Fong, "Tomb-Guardian Figurines: Their Evolution and Iconography," *Ancient Mortuary Traditions of China, papers on Chinese Ceramic Funerary Sculptures*, ed. George Kuwayama (Los Angeles: Far Eastern Art Council, Los Angeles County Museum of Art, 1991), p. 87.
2. Ann Paludan, *The Chinese Spirit Road: The Classical Tradition of Stone Tomb Statuary* (New Haven and London: Yale University Press, 1991), p. 41.
3. Paludan, p. 41.
4. Paludan, p. 42.
5. Fong, p. 92.
6. Fong, p. 92.
7. This and the following have been drawn from Schafer, pp. 85-87; see this work for a more detailed treatment of the lion.
8. See, for example, the carved clouds under the belly of a winged horse at Tailing, tomb of Tang Xuanzong (d. 761) in Shaanxi. Paludan, pp. 105, 108, cat. nos. 132, 135.

10

Probably Shaanxi or Henan province
Tang dynasty (618–907)

CAMEL

(early 8th century)
Earthenware with brown, yellow, green, and transparent lead-fluxed glazes over white slip
32 1/2 in. high (82.6 cm.)
Gift of David K. E. Bruce
BMA 1956.148

This magnificent, striding animal was mold-made and fired twice, once before being glazed and again after at a lower temperature. The use of lead as a flux imparted the brilliance characteristic of the glaze, and lowered the temperature at which it melted, thus necessitating the double firing. The mottling of the blanket was achieved by the use of a resist which derived from similar textile processes found on the batiks imported from Central Asia.

The Chinese were introduced to camels as soon as their sphere of influence expanded westward in the Han dynasty, and during the Tang the government maintained huge herds on the northwest plains.[1] Bactrian camels figured crucially in the trade routes that extended over the vast expanse of southern central Asia through the oasis cities skirting the Takala Makan desert and bordering the Tarim basin. It was possible to transport goods over that vast and inhospitable terrain given the "virtues of the Bactrian camel, which could...predict deadly sandstorms: When such a wind is about to arrive, only the old camels have advance knowledge of it, and they immediately stand snarling together, and bury their mouths in the sand. The men always take this as a sign, and they too immediately cover their noses and mouths by wrapping them in felt...if they did not so protect themselves, they would be in danger of sudden death."[2] Strong camels are able to carry from 500 to 600 pounds and cover about 30 miles a day; some Bactrian camels can transport 1,000 pounds.[3]

These two-humped camels were included in great numbers in the tomb retinues of the time, and in that context are second numerically only to the horse. Symbolically, where pairs of camels have been found, commonly only one was loaded with provisions, typically food, drink, wild game.[4]

1. Wang Zhongshu, p. 58, cites examples of the archeological evidence for the camel which date to the Eastern Han.
2. Schafer, pp. 13–14.
3. *The Columbia Encyclopedia*, 3rd ed. (New York: Columbia University Press, 1967), p. 324.
4. Jacobsen, p. 14.

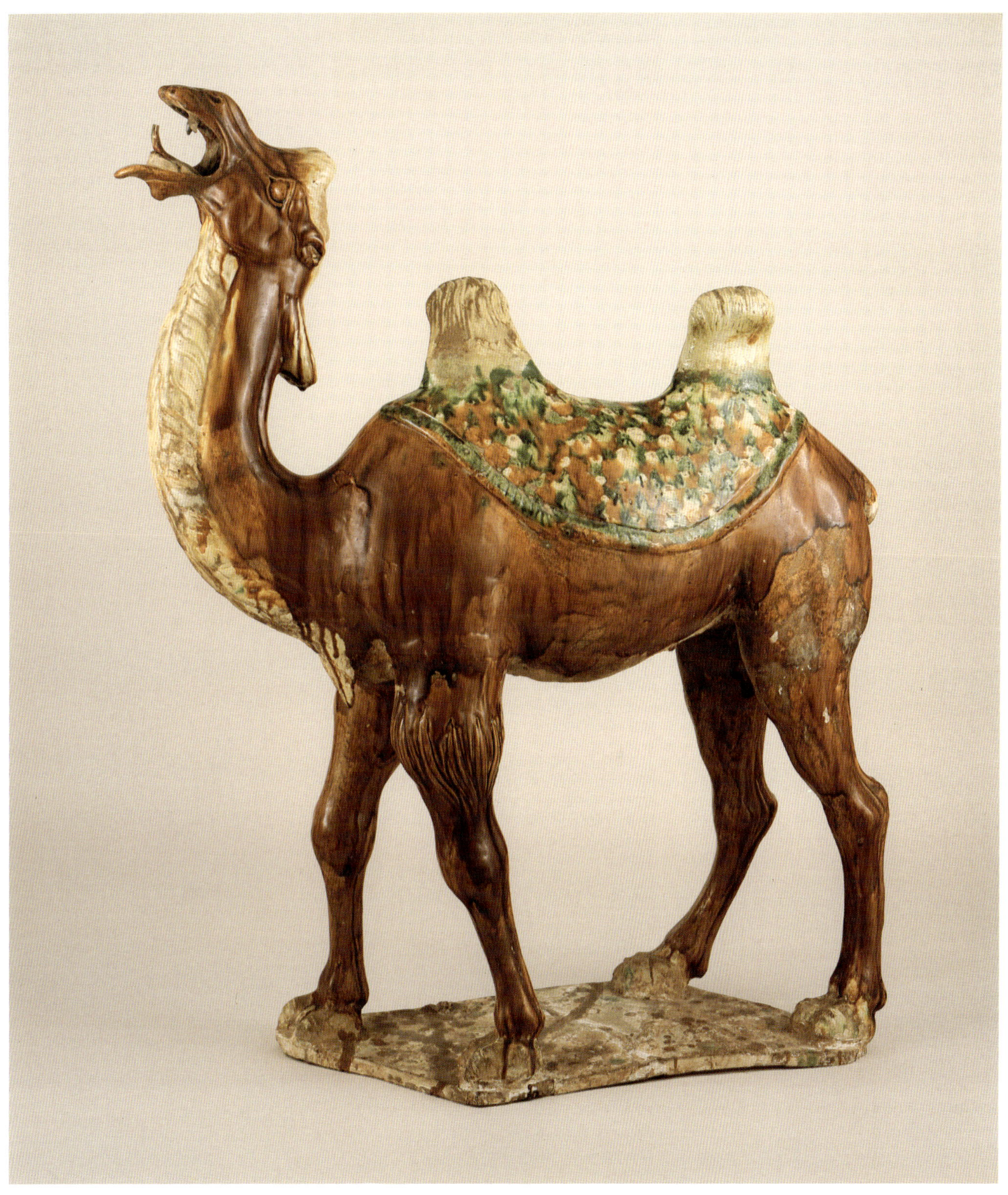

11

Probably Shaanxi or Henan province
Tang dynasty (618–907)

JAR

(early 8th century)
Earthenware with green, amber, and transparent lead-fluxed glazes
7 1/4 in. high (18.5 cm.)
Julius Levy Memorial Fund
BMA 1939.242

Provenance: William H. Whitridge, Baltimore; Ralph M. Chait, New York

Published/Exhibited: Parke-Bernet, New York, November 16–18, 1939, sale 142, lot 266, ill. p. 47; BMA, *A Picture Book*, 1955, ill. p. 90.

A great quantity of "three-color (*sancai*) ware" was produced from the late 7th until the middle 8th century and has been found primarily in the region of the capital, Changan in Shaanxi province as well as Luoyang in Henan province; often, more or fewer than three colors were used. This jar is a good example of a shape common to this ware; furthermore, it displays an uncommonly successful treatment of a difficult glaze technique.

In China in the early Tang period but especially in the capital of Changan, foreign goods were the fashion, and those from the west were most influential. Textiles from Central Asia, including a variety of batiks, were much admired; this jar was glazed by means of a resist, wax, gum, or possibly kaolin powder. After the jar was fired, it was covered first with white slip, and then with a transparent lead-fluxed glaze. On top of this, the resist medium was applied thereby reserving the white petals against the ground of green glaze which was next applied. Lastly, the resist was wiped away from the center of the florettes, and replaced by a daub of yellow glaze. The fact that this technique, which involved a resist-pattern and multiple glazes, was employed on the vertical, rounded surface provides some indication of the high level of skill that was attained in the manufacture of mortuary pottery.

In the area of mortuary pottery the sense of exuberance which seems to have characterized life in the Tang capital is felt not only in sculptural figures of humans and animals but also in ewers, trays, and jars. The simple shape of this jar is animated by the small foot and rounded lip which contain a taut, swelling body. Although there are a number of similar jars with accompanying lids, so many have been found without them that it seems unlikely that all had lids originally.[1]

1. Watson, p. 112.

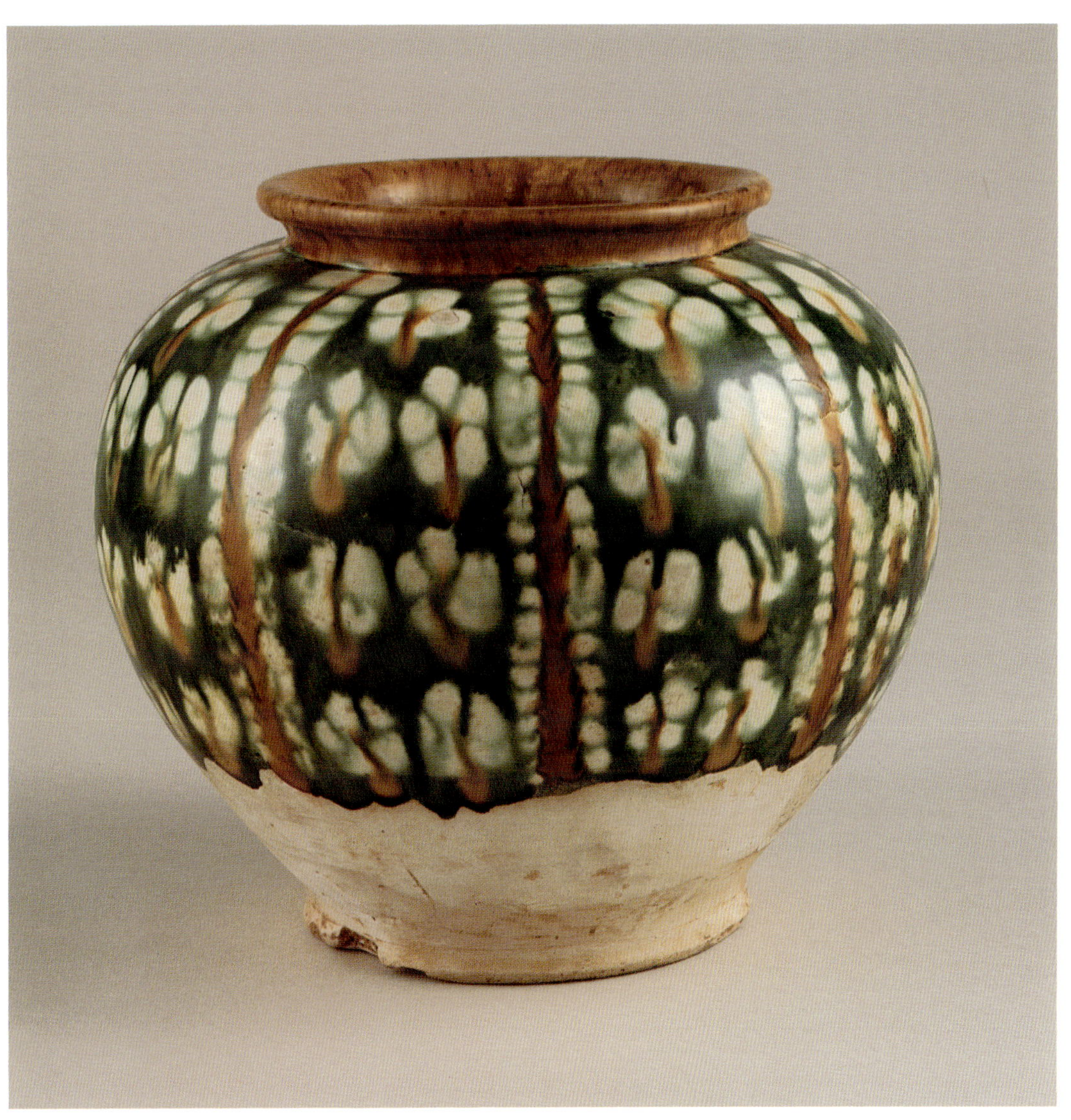

12

Probably Henan province
Tang dynasty (618–907)

JAR

(8th century)
Earthenware with blue and amber lead-fluxed glazes
5 3/8 in. high (13.7 cm.)
Julius Levy Memorial Fund
BMA 1939.247

Provenance: William H. Whitridge, Baltimore

Published/Exhibited: BMA, *The Whitridge Collection of Chinese Pottery and Porcelain*, June 1–October 15, 1930, p. 68, no. 238; Parke-Bernet, New York, November 16–18, 1939, sale 142, lot 238.

13

Probably Henan province
Tang dynasty (618–907)

CUP

Fine white earthenware with green, amber, and transparent lead-fluxed glazes over white slip
3 3/8 in. diam. (8.5 cm.)
Gift of Lawrason Riggs of J
BMA 1945.59.14

Provenance: Ralph M. Chait, New York

14

Tang dynasty (618–907)-Song dynasty (960–1279)

LARGE CUP

(10th century?)
Earthenware with degraded bright green lead-fluxed glaze
3 13/16 in. high (9.7 cm.)
Julius Levy Memorial Fund
BMA 1939.243

Provenance: William H. Whitridge, Baltimore

Published/Exhibited: BMA, *The Whitridge Collection of Chinese Pottery and Porcelain*, June 1–October 15, 1930, p. 85, no. 317; Parke-Bernet, New York, November 16–18, 1939, sale 142, lot 267.

15

Probably Henan province
Tang dynasty (618–907)

SHALLOW BOWL

(8th century)
Earthenware with
blue lead glaze
4 1/2 in. diam. (11.4 cm.)
Gift of Lawrason Riggs of J
BMA 1945.59.16

Provenance: Ralph M. Chait, New York

Metal forms inspired numerous mortuary pottery copies, such as these three cups; moreover one cup and the jar document the early use of cobalt oxide as a coloring agent.

Dark blue, from cobalt oxide, was used less often than green or brown in glazing Tang dynasty pottery. Imported from the West in the form of glass, it was the most expensive of the glaze pigments. There was, not surprisingly, some experimentation with underglaze-painted cobalt decoration during the Tang dynasty but it was not until the 14th century, and coupled with porcelain, that this means was regularly employed.[1] Both the jar and the cup display a characteristically taut profile. An amber streak further embellishes the jar.[2]

The particularly graceful form of the deep cup is emphasized by the application of the runny green and amber glazes in streaks down its side; this type is thought to be somewhat later in date than those with resist decoration.[3] The earthenware body of the cup is very white, but was still coated with slip which provided a smoother surface.

The large, leaf-green cup represents the continuation of the tradition of low-fired, lead-glazed mortuary pottery beyond its height in the early 8th century. The pink clay body is relatively soft; the glaze thinly applied, watery, and degraded by burial moisture.

1. Wu Tung and Denise Patry Leidy, "Recent Archaeological Contributions to the Study of Chinese Ceramics," in *Imperial Taste: Chinese Ceramics from the Percival David Foundation* (Los Angeles: Los Angeles County Museum of Art and San Francisco: Chronicle Books, 1989), p. 98.
2. A similar jar with a higher neck is in the Yale University Art Gallery (1947.77). It also is glazed yellow in the interior with yellow streaks in the blue glaze; moreover, it has two small blisters at the shoulder line. See Lee, p. 22, no. 31. An unusual feature of the BMA jar is the presence of the two unglazed patches on opposite sides of the shoulder, which appear to result from a glazing accident rather than kiln flaw.
3. Watson, p. 20.

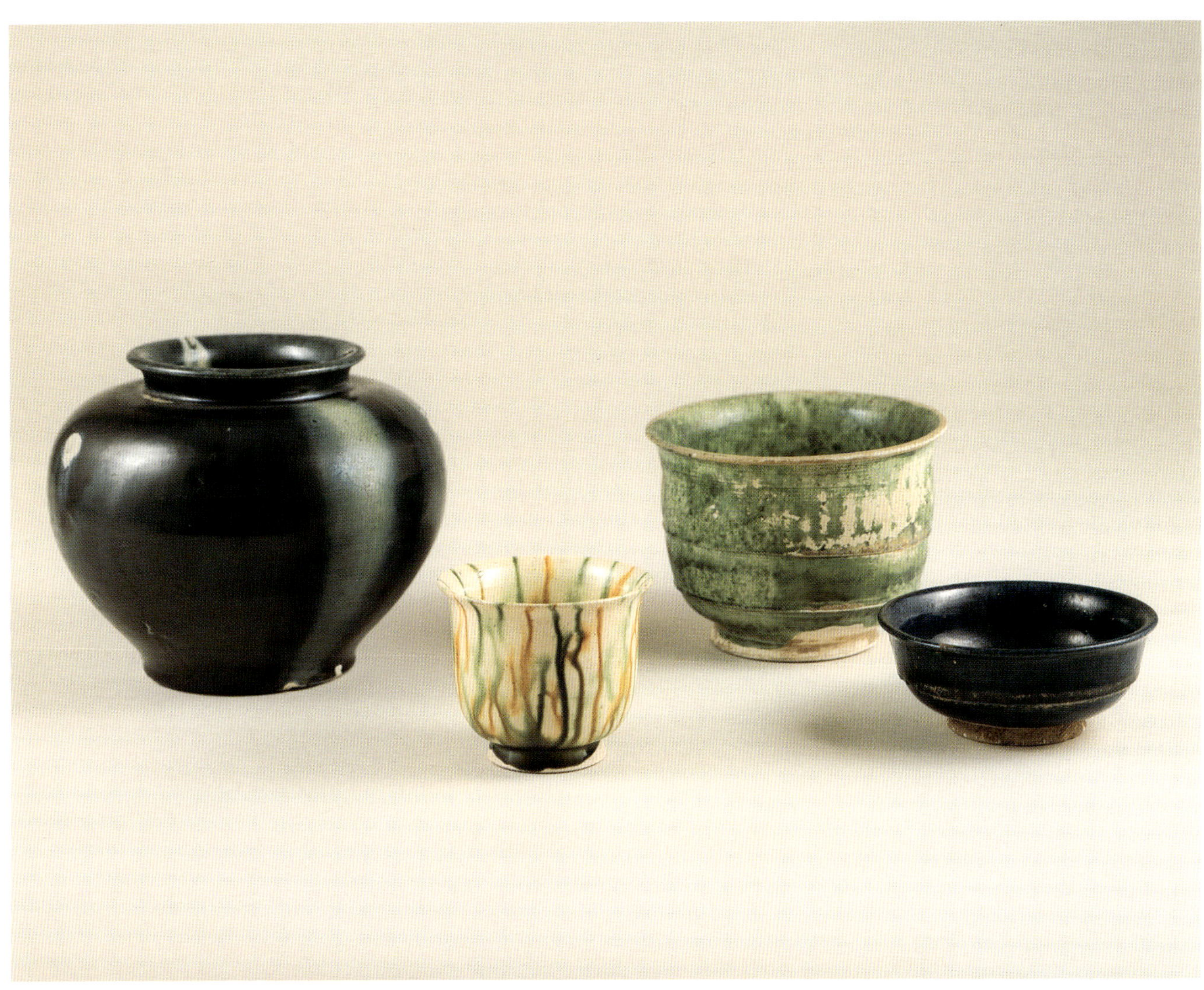

12, 13, 14, 15

16

Henan or Hebei province
Tang dynasty (618–907)

STEM CUP

(late 7th–early 8th century)
Fine white stoneware with transparent, greenish glaze
2 13/16 in. high (7.2 cm.)
Frank J. and Elizabeth L. Goodnow Collection, by exchange
BMA 1989.78

Provenance: Andrew Kahane, Limited, New York; Helner Collection, Stockholm

17

Henan or Hebei province
Tang dynasty (618–907)

SMALL "AMBROSIA" FORM VASE

(8th century)
Porcelain with transparent glaze
5 1/2 in. high (14 cm.)
Gift of Terri and Erwin Harris, Baltimore
BMA 1987.288

Provenance: Warren Cox Collection, New York

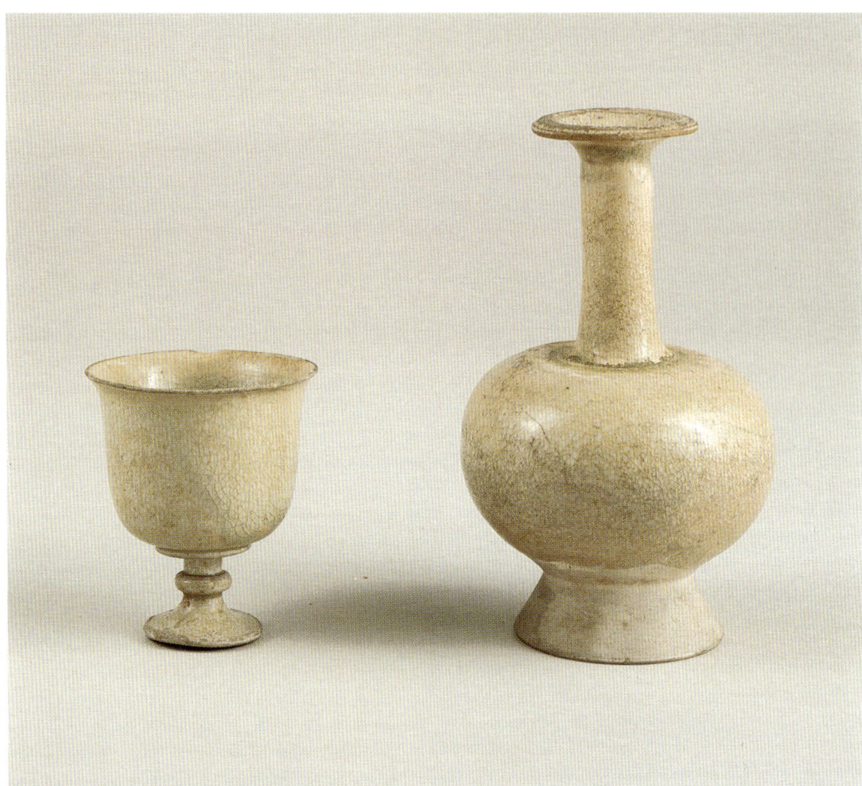

During the Shang dynasty (c. 16th–11th century B.C.), Chinese potters worked with white-firing clays which were quite brittle and therefore extremely fragile. Early in the 6th century, white-glazed wares appeared again; this time, the combination of clays along with two further technical advances resulted in durable stoneware.[1] By mid-century, the northern stoneware tradition was well established; indeed, a concentrated development of the ware is suggested by substantial finds recovered from late 6th and early 7th-century tombs. These whitewares led rapidly to the development of porcelain during the Tang dynasty (618–907).[2]

Before the end of the Sui dynasty (581–618), whitewares presumably began to replace the lacquer, silver, and bronze vessels used in wealthy households.[3] In fact, both of these delicate objects derive from metal prototypes.[4] The vase originated in a Buddhist context, where it is frequently shown held by bodhisattvas; it takes its name from the elixir of life or ambrosia which it contained.

1. Margaret Medley, *T'ang Pottery and Porcelain* (London: Faber and Faber, 1981), p. 67, discusses its characteristics—grayish-white or buff-colored body of variable density but hard, covered with transparent greenish-yellow, yellow, or brown glaze—and calls attention to the fact that the unglazed body rarely shows any oxidation, a result of good kiln control and the probable use of saggers; Juliano refers to tombs datable to 575, 595, and 608 from Hebei and Henan.
2. Traditionally, porcelain has been defined in the West as being white, translucent, vitrified, and resonant when struck. It is distinguishable from stoneware on the basis of its whiteness and translucence. The two types of high-fired wares are separated by degrees: a coarse clay fired to a sufficiently high temperature will result in porcelain, while a fine clay fired to a lower temperature may produce stoneware. The Chinese differentiate only between low-fired (earthenware) and high-fired (stoneware, porcelain) clay bodies.
3. Medley, p. 68.
4. The Museum is fortunate to possess a comparable contemporary gilt-bronze stem cup (BMA 1991.214).

18

Five Dynasties period (907–960)

STORAGE JAR (MEIPING)

(early 10th century)
Porcelain with transparent glaze over white slip
6 1/4 in. high (15.9 cm.)
Julius Levy Memorial Fund
BMA 1988.67

Provenance: J. J. Lally & Co., New York; Alfred and Ivy Clark Collection, London; Diedrich Abbes Collection, New York (on loan to the BMA, 1929–1931)

Published/Exhibited: Warren E. Cox, *The Book of Pottery and Porcelain*, New York, Lothrop Lee and Shepard Co., Inc., Crown Publishers, 1944, vol. 1, ill. p. 117, pl. 32; Oriental Ceramics Society, London, *Arts of the Tang Dynasty*, February 25–March 30, 1955, no. 224; Oriental Ceramics Society, London, *Arts of the Sung Dynasty*, June 16–July 23, 1960, no. 120.

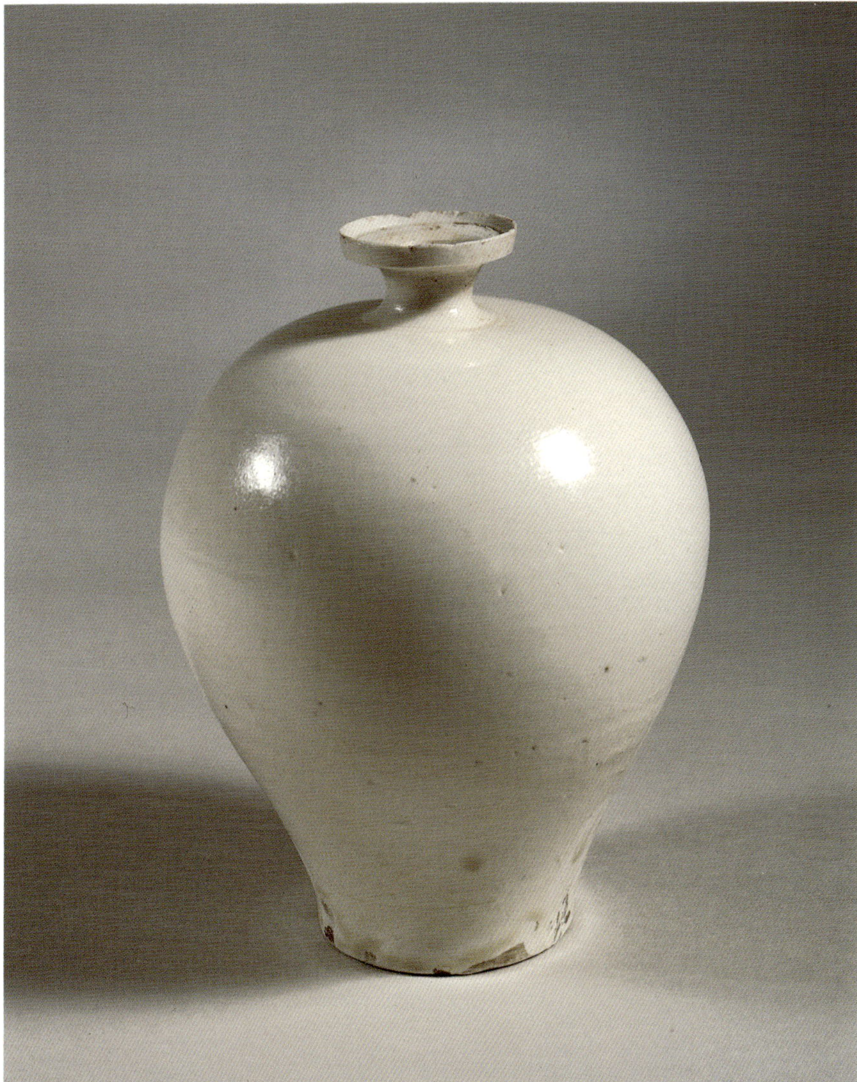

During the 10th century, whitewares were produced generally throughout north China, some were porcelains and some stonewares.[1] Slip was used on both types, to mask imperfections in the clay body. The transparent glaze which covers the vase exhibits the dark streaks associated with Ding ware; however, the shape more closely resembles Cizhou pieces. The vase is essentially transitional in nature; its exaggerated profile recalls Tang dynasty flamboyance, yet its balanced form and plain surface anticipate Song dynasty restraint.

The descriptive name, *meiping* (literally, plum vase), refers to a vessel with a small mouth, a short and slender neck, rounded shoulders, and a narrow foot with no visible foot ring; it was adopted during the Qing dynasty. This vessel was intended to hold a liquid of some type; the way the mouth is finished "probably had something to do with the sealing and covering methods" used at the time.[2]

1. The porcelains were obtained from the local kaolinic clays without the addition of porcelain stone; see Valenstein, p. 92. The stonewares are associated principally with the Cizhou tradition that flourished in the north.
2. Tregear, p. 22.

19

Henan province, Huangdao kilns
Tang dynasty (618–907)

JAR DECORATED WITH PETAL-FORM SPLASHES

(8th century)
Buff stoneware with dark brown glaze with bluish-gray suffused splashes
6 5/16 in. diam. (16 cm.)
Purchase with exchange funds from Gift of Howard C. Hollis
BMA 1991.31

Provenance: J. J. Lally & Co., New York; Private Collection, Holland

This stout jar is decorated with a variegated glaze effect perhaps inspired by the lead-glazed mortuary pottery of the time. The suffused-glaze wares of north China are considered the precursors of the blue-glazed Jun wares produced primarily in Henan after the 11th century. The Japanese call the whitish blue-gray glaze, which has been splashed over the dark ground, "sea-slug" (*namako*);[1] the Chinese call a similar ware from Dundian kilns, "flowery stoneware" (*huaci*).[2] The splashes on this jar have been applied deliberately around the rim and as five petals around the body. The degree of control is noteworthy and accentuates the girth of the body.

1. Watson, p. 62.
2. Lu Yaw, p. 32.

20

Probably Henan province, Jun ware kilns
Jin dynasty (1115–1234)

DEEP BOWL

(12th century)
Stoneware with bright blue glaze
6 1/2 in. diam. (16.5 cm.)
Purchase with exchange funds from The Mary Frick Jacobs Collection
BMA 1991.120

Provenance: Andrew Kahane, Limited, New York; Anthony R. Derham, New York; Mrs. Charles B. Scully; Samuel T. Peters, New York

Published/Exhibited: S. C. Bosch Reitz, *Exhibition of Early Chinese Pottery and Sculpture*, New York, The Metropolitan Museum of Art, 1916, ill. no. 117.

The bowl is covered with a bright, even blue glaze which has pulled away from the mouth in an uneven line and stops just above the foot rim; both mouth and foot oxidized in the firing to a dark reddish-brown.[1] Chips in the rim, and normal abrasion on the bottom of the foot reveal the fine, gray stoneware body. The full bowl tapers very slightly at the mouth and is sharply contracted above the medium-high, tapered foot ring. The interior of the foot is glazed.

The bright blue color and pleasing proportions of this object are features associated with a ware known as Jun, from its ostensible origin at Juntai in Henan.[2] At a time when stonewares were covered with white, black, or grayish-green glazes, Jun wares were quite singularly colorful. The beautiful ranges of blue resulted from the "spontaneous unmixing" of the glaze components, lime and silica, in such a way that minute bubbles trapped within the glaze reflect light toward the blue end of the spectrum; the effect was enhanced by multiple glaze layers and reduction firings followed by slow cooling.[3]

While in many respects it exhibits the finest qualities of Jun ware, nevertheless, this lovely, large bowl remains something of an anomaly by virtue of its unglazed rim from which the glaze has pulled away in an uneven line. It would most likely have had a lid originally.

1. There is some evidence of biscuit-firing and the application of a ferruginous slip or dressing beneath the glaze of Jun wares. This bowl has no such dressing; in conversation with Margaret Medley, April 6, 1992.
2. Lu Yaw, p. 32.
3. *Iron in the Fire*, p. 13.

21

Possibly Shaanxi province, Yaozhou kilns
or Henan province, Baofeng kiln
Northern Song dynasty (960–1127)

FOLIATE VASE

(11th century)
Stoneware with olive-green glaze
5 5/16 in. high (13.5 cm.)
Gift of Fred J. van Slyke
BMA 1964.53.2

The kilns of China did not operate in isolation, each producing a single, unique product. On the contrary, certain kilns were especially influential, and a number of popular wares were widely copied. A good example of a ware which inspired many copies and was itself derived from another is the northern celadon produced by the Yaozhou kilns of Shaanxi province. These stonewares, made from the 11th until the 13th century and characterized by a fine gray body with a bright, clear olive-green glaze and first carved, later molded decoration, were made in imitation of the fine gray-green celadon from northern Zhejiang province, which was sent during the 10th century to the Northern Song capital of Kaifeng in Henan province from the ancient kingdom Yue.[1] Many northern kilns produced similar, if generally inferior, celadon ware. Coal was used to fire this ware in a reducing atmosphere in single chamber, domed kilns. Northern celadon clay contains about twice as much iron as its southern counterpart at Longquan, hence the darker color of the ware. The "speckled blemish" on the glaze is typical.[2]

Based on a metal prototype, this foliate vase is composed of four disparate elements. Its high foot is undecorated; its lower body is squat, rounded, and decorated with an abstracted, if not somewhat crude, peony scroll while its upper body is tall and cylindrical, flaring somewhat at the top and bottom; its lip is composed of six, sharply everted petals given greater definition by six plain lines in the interior. The abstracted, serrated-edge leaf motif decorating the upper body is completely vertical, in contrast to which the peony scroll has strong diagonals. Although similar vases have been attributed to the Yaozhou kilns, the stiffness of the upright leaves has parallels with a shard found at one of the kilns in Henan province.[3]

According to unverified information from the donor, the vase "was formerly owned by Prince Qing who was one of the most powerful men during the last part of the Qing dynasty" and "was excavated from a tomb in Henan province in the latter part of the 18th century."

1. Tregear, in Lu Yaw, p. 41.
2. Tregear, p. 102.
3. For a similar example in the Metropolitan Museum collection, Valenstein cites three comparable examples from the Yaozhou kilns of Shaanxi; a shard with the same distinctive stylized, serrated-edge petal design from Henan, Baofeng, was included in Hughes-Stanton and Kerr. This vase is most similar to one at the Yale University Art Gallery (1955.4.6) which nevertheless differs in having a pierced foot and a plain foliate rim.

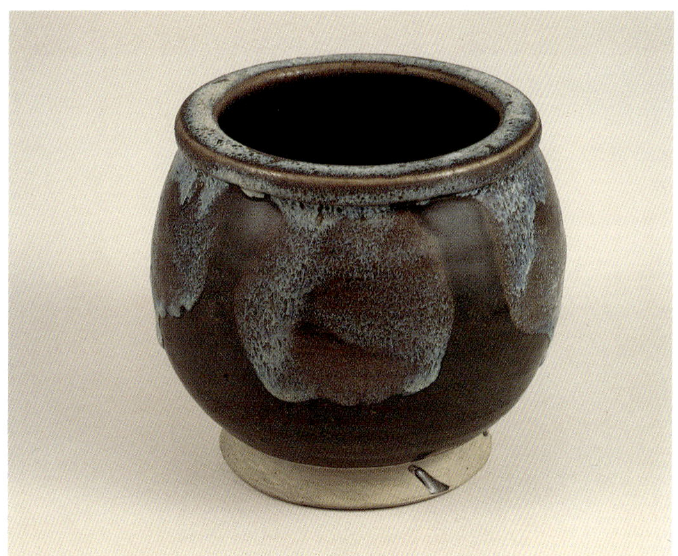

19

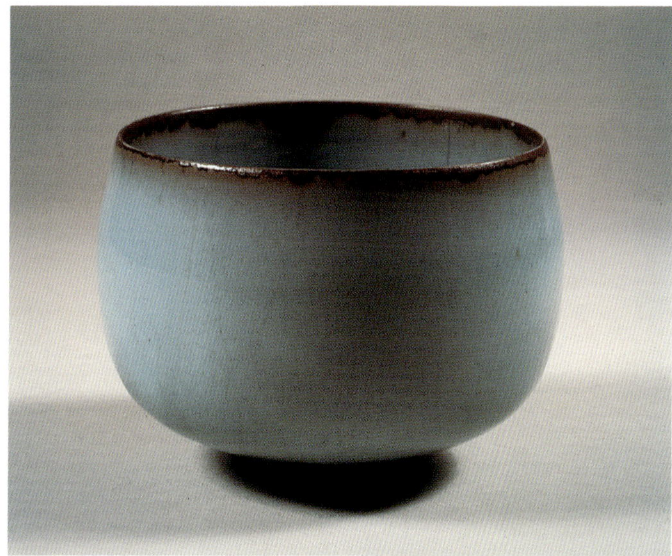

20

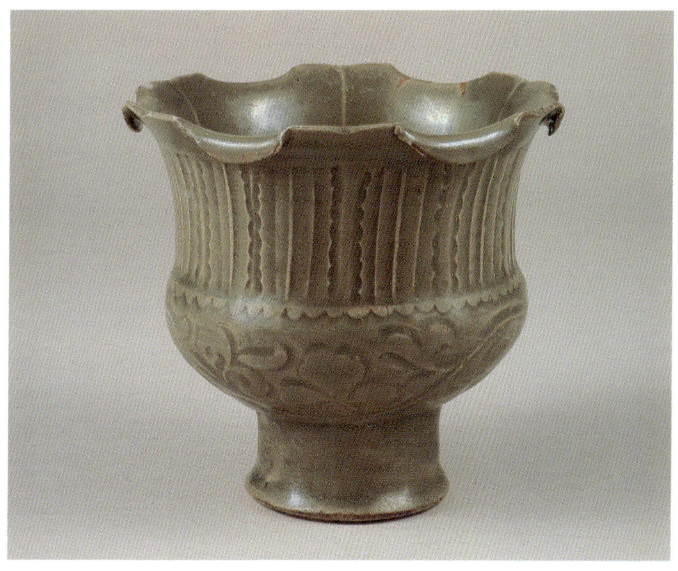

21

22

Zhejiang province, Longquan kilns
Southern Song dynasty (1127–1279)

DRAGON VASE

(12th century)
Stoneware with celadon glaze
7 1/16 in. high (18 cm.)
Julius Levy Memorial Fund
BMA 1939.249

Provenance: William H. Whitridge, Baltimore

Published/Exhibited: BMA, *The Whitridge Collection of Chinese Pottery and Porcelain*, June 1–October 15, 1930, p. 104, no. 434, ill.; Parke-Bernet, New York, November 16–18, 1939, sale 142, lot 434; Walters Art Gallery, "Chinese Ceramics," April 30–September 15, 1956.

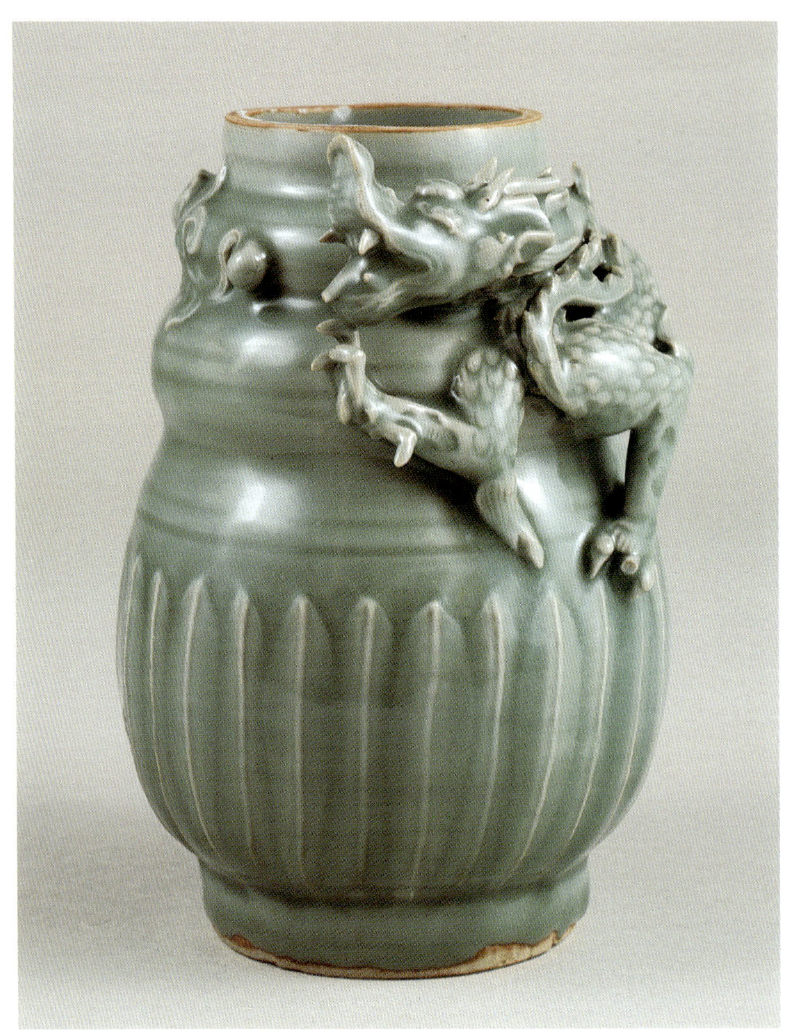

This funerary vase is a product of the Longquan kilns in southeastern Zhejiang province.[1] Originating during the late Tang dynasty and continuing well into the Ming, the kilns produced what is termed classic celadon during the Southern Song to early 14th century.[2] In producing its distinctive celadon, Longquan artisans drew upon both southern and northern greenware traditions, specifically the perfectly matched stoneware bodies and green glazes of Yue ware and the undecorated unctuous surfaces epitomized by Ru ware.[3]

In contrast to its northern counterpart, Longquan celadon was made of a pale gray, almost white, stoneware. The green glaze was lighter and also thicker, opaque rather than transparent.[4] It was especially well suited for applied and carved decoration, such as the exceptionally vigorous dragon, modeled by hand, encircling the shoulder and the upright petals decorating the body of this vase.

1. Cremation was widely practiced in southern China, and a number of similar covered urns have been found to contain bones.
2. Tregear, p.178, is more specific in regard to the later date, "first quarter of the 14th century."
3. Tregear, p. 168.
4. Nigel Wood, in *Iron in the Fire*, p. 52, discusses the composition of these jade-like, lime-alkali glazes.

23

Zhejiang province, Longquan kilns
Southern Song period (1127–1279)

TRIPOD CENSER

(13th century)
Fine stoneware with blue-green celadon glaze
6 in. wide (15.3 cm.)
Gift of Howard C. Hollis, by exchange
BMA 1988.649

Provenance: J. J. Lally & Co., New York

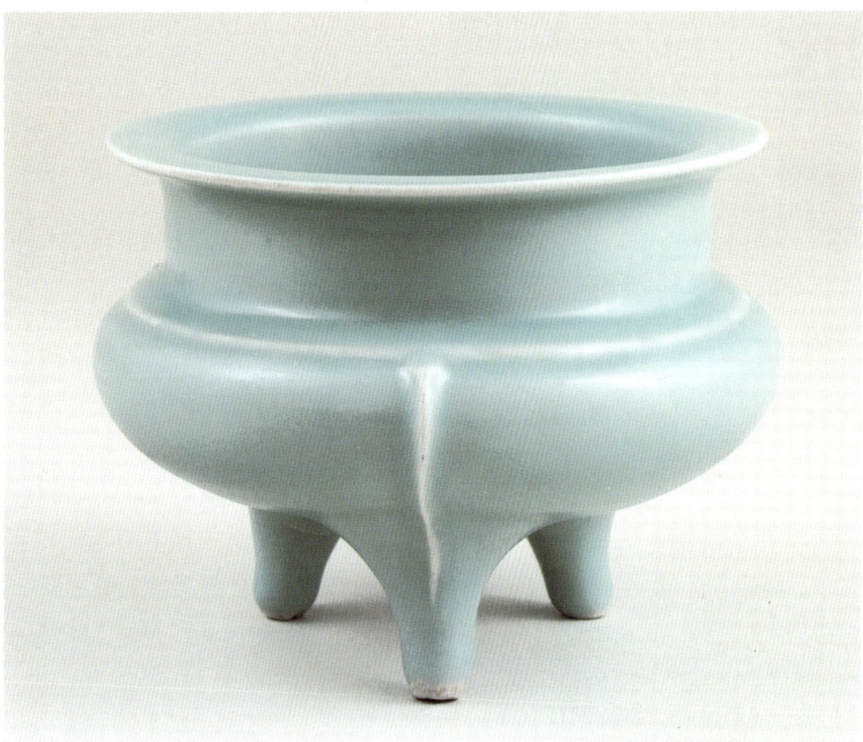

Whereas northern celadons were fired in single-chamber kilns, the southern wares were fired in multichambered kilns, known as dragon kilns, which typically extended up a hillside at a gentle slope. The division of the long kiln into separate chambers allowed greater control of the firing cycle as well as increased capacity. One kiln at Jincun measured some 50 meters long and was estimated to have accommodated 170 packed saggers standing 15 high in each of 8 chambers for a total capacity on the order of 25,000 for a single firing.[1]

The date of this object reflects the recovery of cargo from a merchant ship which sank in 1323 off the coast of Sinan, South Korea, believed to have been on its way to Japan. As of September 1982, almost 18,000 articles were salvaged, of which over 16,000 were pottery and of that number 9,600 were celadons.[2] Well-represented among those celadons was this shape.

The censer, or incense burner, would have been filled with sand on which pieces of incense were placed or into which were stuck incense sticks. The form, characteristically simple and well-balanced, is distinguished by a fine, pale gray body and bright, blue-green glaze.[3] This tripod incense burner illustrates perfectly the accomplishment of Longquan potters in maintaining a high level of quality while producing tremendous quantities of greatly-admired celadons. However, that balance ultimately could not be sustained, and whether due to increased output, depletion of the finest clay, or both, the quality of Longquan wares did decline soon after the 13th century.

1. Gompertz, p. 162.
2. Valenstein, pp. 124 and 137.
3. The glaze color is called *kinuta* by the Japanese, and plum green or powder green by the Chinese according to Lu Yaw, p. 4.

24

Probably Shanxi province, Datong kilns
Jin dynasty (1115–1234)

VASE WITH CUT-GLAZE LOTUS FLOWER AND LEAF DESIGN

(13th century)
Buff stoneware with dark brown slip glaze
9 1/2 in. high (24.1 cm.)
Purchase with exchange funds from Gift of Howard C. Hollis, and Bequest of Saidie A. May
BMA 1990.156

Provenance: Eskenazi Limited, London; Rudolph Schaeffer, San Francisco; Warren E. Cox, New York; Samuel T. Peters, New York

Published/Exhibited: Warren E. Cox, *The Book of Pottery and Porcelain*, New York, Lothrop Lee and Shepard Co., Crown Publishers, 1944, vol. 1, pp. 174–180, ill. p. 177, pl. 52.

The Cizhou kilns of northern China produced a range of boldly decorated, utilitarian stonewares over a long period of time, beginning in the late Tang dynasty (618–907) and continuing to the present day. The decorative techniques associated with these wares include incising, sgraffito, cut-glaze carving, underglaze painting in iron oxides, and overglaze painting in multicolored lead-fluxed enamels. The kilns at Cizhou were the first to employ in the 12th century colorful, low-fired enamels on high-fired objects, and this was achieved by two firings at the requisite different temperatures, a practice which originated with Tang dynasty mortuary pottery.

Cizhou wares are characterized by strong black-white decoration, often achieved by the use of slip, a thin mixture of clay and water, beneath a transparent, black or brown glaze. This slip served to obscure imperfections in the clay body; decoratively, it provided a contrast with the glaze, or a ground for painted decoration. Less commonly, a dark glaze, used alone, was cut away so that as on this vase the light clay body stands out against the rich brown glaze.

The motifs that decorate these sturdy wares include a variety of floral and foliate scrolls, birds, fish, animals, and figural scenes. The shapes were utilitarian (jars, vases, bowls, pillows), and tended to be larger than items made by the comparable southern kilns at Jizhou. It has been suggested that craftsmen from Cizhou relocated to Jizhou when the Song court moved to the south in the 13th century to escape the invading Jurchen tribe which established the Jin dynasty.

Like the plum blossom which is found on the Jizhou jar (BMA 1989.77), the lotus is weighted with meaning and allusion. It is a symbol of Buddhism, for "its fruits are said to be ripe when the flower blooms, just as the truth preached by Buddha bears immediately the fruit of enlightenment."[1] It can also represent purity undefiled by the mire from which it grows, and, for its many seeds, fertility. The lotus is as well cultivated agriculturally for its edible seeds and root. It is highly regarded for its beauty and utility, as are the wares from Cizhou, hence its choice as decoration for this vase is especially appropriate.

1. C.A.S. Williams, *Dictionary of Chinese Art Motives* (New York: Dover Press, 1982), p. 257.

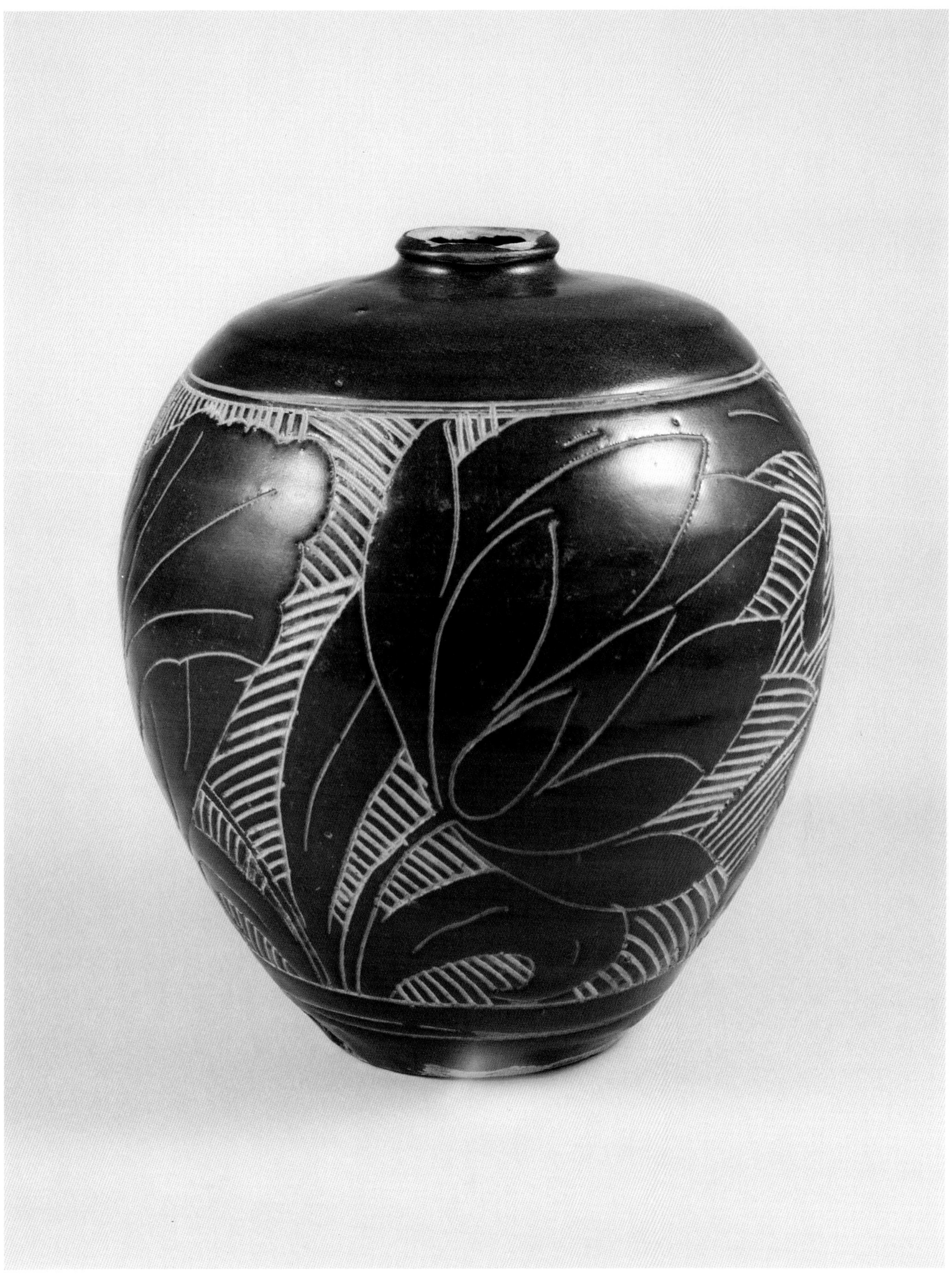

25

Jiangxi province, Jizhou kilns
Southern Song (1127–1279)-Yuan dynasty (1271–1368)

JAR WITH BISCUIT-RESERVED PLUM BLOSSOMS

(13th century)
Stoneware with dark brown glaze over dressing
9 9/16 in. high (24.3 cm.)
Julius Levy Memorial Fund, by exchange
BMA 1989.77

Provenance: J. J. Lally & Co., New York

The kilns at Jizhou in Jiangxi province to the south and west of Jingdezhen produced utilitarian stonewares, imaginatively decorated often by means of some resist, generally with a leaf or paper cut-out, though probably also with wax or clay. The blossoms decorating this sturdy jar were obtained by the placement of paper patterns on the surface before it was covered with an iron-rich dressing and then glazed. The deep brown of the glaze is obtained by the addition of manganese oxide to the iron oxide in the glaze and dressing.[1]

Images of the plum blossom proliferated on decorative objects as well as in poetry and painting during the Southern Song. The symbol of regeneration, early flowering and simple beauty, attracted a cult following devoted to discovering the flower in a multitude of settings, enjoying it, and experiencing it completely. "'Searching for plum blossoms'—the quest to catch the very first moment of spring—took many forms. Alone with a servant or in the company of friends, literati made moonlit excursions in pursuit of plum blossoms, seeking them in the wilds of mountains and at watersides or in the depths of country estates. Sometimes on foot through snow, sometimes in boats on lake or stream—always it seems with wine—they sought the subtle fragrance and fleeting beauty of the blossoms."[2]

The embodiment of understated beauty, plum blossoms are used as effectively on delicate white porcelains as on sturdy black stonewares, such as this jar.

1. Nigel Wood in *Iron in the Fire*, p. 14.
2. Bickford, p. 28.

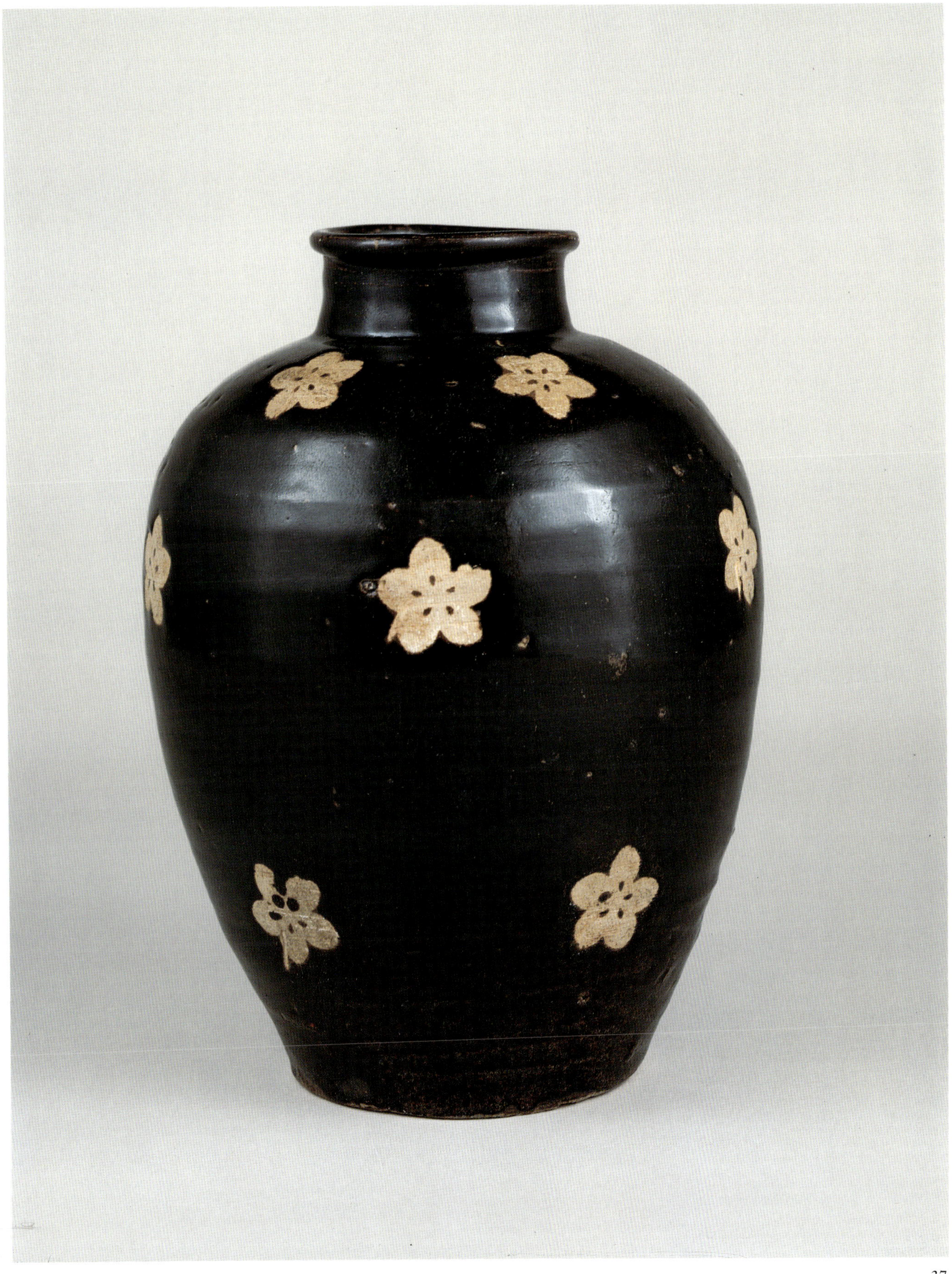

26

Jiangxi province, Jingdezhen kilns, Qingbai ware
Southern Song period (1127–1279)

BOWL

(12th–13th century)
Porcelain with transparent glaze, rim bound with copper
8 1/8 in. diam. (20.6 cm.)
Julius Levy Memorial Fund
BMA 1952.9

Provenance: Howard C. Hollis, Cleveland

Published/Exhibited: Walters Art Gallery, "Chinese Ceramics," April 30–September 15, 1956.

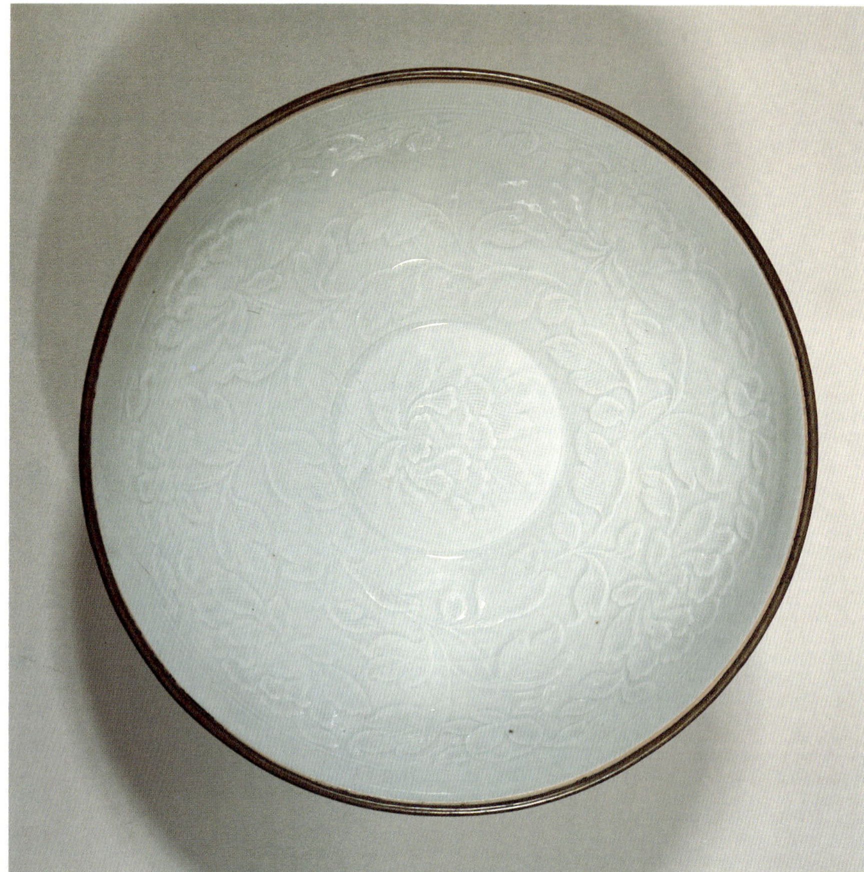

By the 13th century the area around Jingdezhen in Jiangxi province had become and would remain China's preeminent center for the production of porcelain. As had other major kiln sites, Jingdezhen had access to the essentials of water transportation, a ready fuel supply, and most importantly, raw materials.

These materials were a rather unique form of porcelain stone which possessed an unusual degree of plasticity and could thus be used alone, and a sedimentary china clay or kaolin especially free of iron and high in alumina.[1] By the 13th century potters at Jingdezhen were combining small amounts of kaolin with the porcelain stone. The subsequent development of porcelain reflects an ever greater percentage of kaolin as well as the use of other types of clay.[2]

Methods of decorating the Qingbai porcelain of Jingdezhen evolved in accordance with past models, such as northern celadon and especially Ding wares. Initially embellished with carved motifs and fired upright, by the later 12th and 13th century Qingbai bowls generally were fired upside down to reduce warpage as well as increase the capacity of the kiln, and often decorated by means of a mold.[3] Once thrown, the bowl was placed over a mold and was shaved to the proper degree of thinness. The beautiful peony design relates to contemporary brocades, and based on the large size of the flowers, the treatment of the buds, and the denseness of the design, may be indicative of a later date.[4]

1. The name derives from gaolin, the term used by the Chinese for the far hills from which the stone came.
2. Valenstein, p. 312.
3. As a result of the combined technique of molding and firing upside down, the size of the foot ring is greatly decreased. In addition, these porcelains of the later 12th and 13th centuries were not always completely dry when they were fired. The moisture resulted in a faintly yellowish cast to the glaze, in contrast to the very blue glaze of earlier objects; J. M. Addis, *Jingdezhen Wares: The Yuan Evolution* (Hong Kong: Oriental Ceramic Society of Hong Kong, 1984), p. 13.
4. The bowl could even date into the 14th century; Margaret Medley, in conversation, April 6, 1992.

27

Jiangxi province, Jingdezhen kilns
Yuan dynasty (1271–1368)

FOLIATE-FORM CUP WITH STAND

(early 14th century)
Porcelain with transparent glaze
.a) cup: 2 15/16 in. diam. (7.4 cm.); .b) stand: 5 15/16 in. diam. (15 cm.), slightly irregular
Gift of Peter and Irene Scheinman, New York
BMA 1991.344a-b

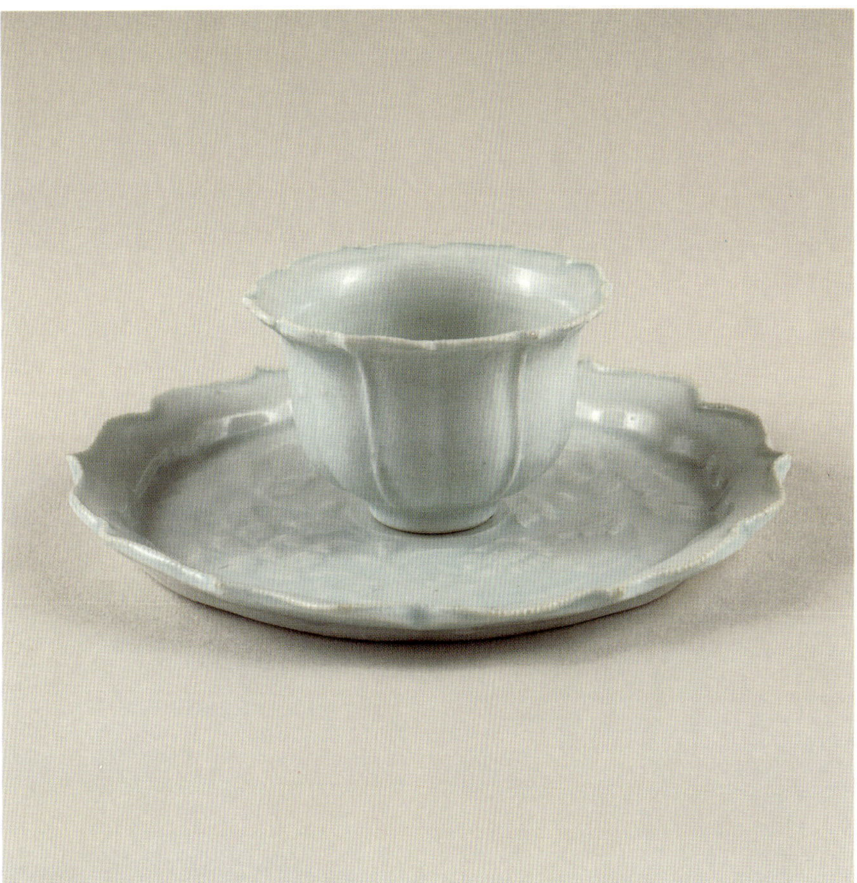

This rare and beautiful cup with stand, fashioned of fine, white porcelain and covered with a bright, bluish transparent glaze, belongs to a group of porcelains characterized by beaded decoration and produced from the late 13th until the mid-14th century. Buddhist figures, vases, and smaller, coarser articles mainly exported to Southeast Asia, are related by virtue of this type of trimming.

The Buddhist figures, wearing beaded jewelry and other applied ornaments, have been especially helpful in establishing a chronology. One small Guanyin was found in a tomb datable to 1274, while the Water Moon Guanyin at the Nelson-Atkins Museum is dated by inscription to 1298 or 1299. Also included in the group is the famous Fonthill vase, with its beaded openwork floral panels, now in the National Museum of Ireland, which was given by Louis the Great of Hungary to Charles III of Durazzo in 1381 and remains the earliest documented piece of Chinese porcelain to have reached Europe.

Toward the end of the 13th century, the potteries at Jingdezhen began to experiment with the kinds of clay used to produce porcelain. Recent studies indicate that initially their porcelain was produced with a unique form of kaolinized porcelain stone (or petuntse);[1] limestone was added to this to obtain the Qingbai glaze which from its iron content assumed the bluish color in a reduction atmosphere. Later, a different type of porcelain stone was combined with china clay (kaolin), necessitating a higher firing temperature but resulting in a stronger body. It has been theorized that the addition of the kaolin made increased sizes possible, and was indeed prompted by a specific desire to obtain large votive figures.[2] The survival of this cup with its original stand, the delicate barbs of both intact, is a powerful argument for the evolving strength of porcelain at this time.

1. That is, porcelain stone having some of the properties of kaolin as a result of a high percentage of mica contained within it; see Margaret Medley, "Techniques and Style in Qingbai Decoration from Southern Song to Ming," in *Jingdezhen Wares: The Yuan Evolution* (Hong Kong: The Oriental Ceramic Society of Hong Kong and Fung Ping Shan Museum, University of Hong Kong, 1984), p. 23.
2. Medley, pp. 25–26.

28

Jiangxi province, Jingdezhen kilns
Yuan (1271–1368)-Ming dynasty (1368–1644)

VASE

(late 14th century)
Porcelain with underglaze cobalt decoration
11 5/16 in. high (28.7 cm.)
Julius Levy Memorial Fund
BMA 1959.45

Provenance: Howard C. Hollis, Cleveland

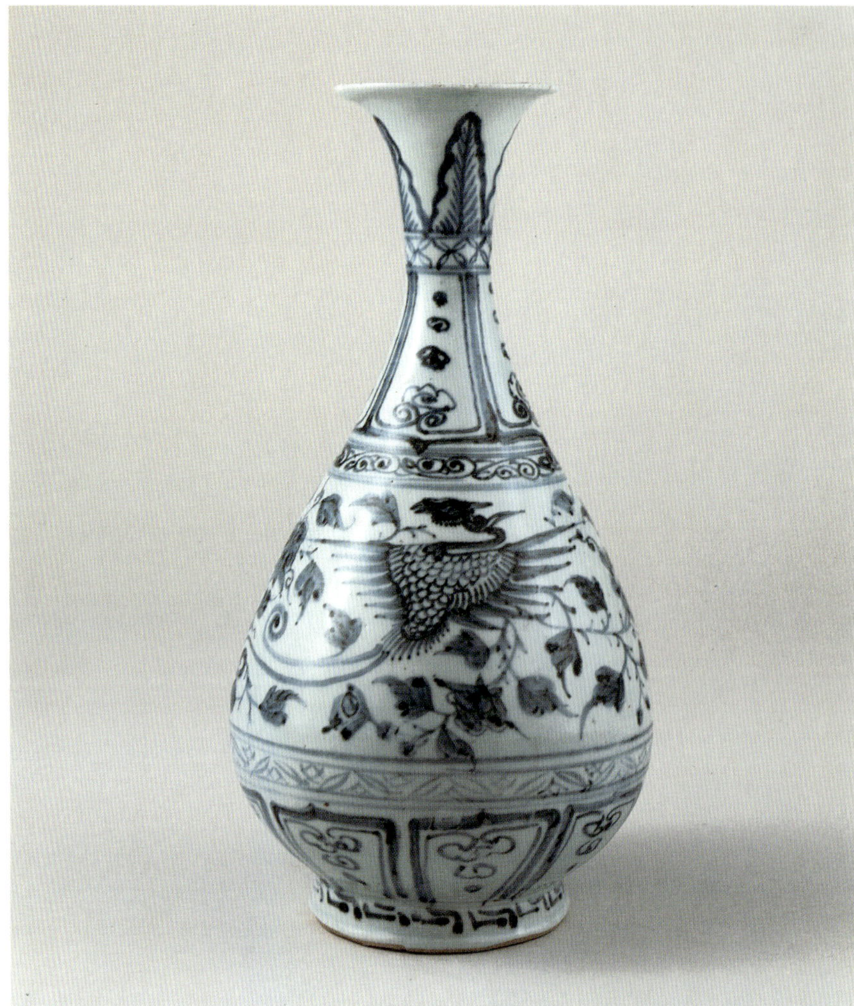

Not used in quantity since the Tang dynasty when it was most likely imported in the form of glass, the reappearance of cobalt has traditionally been attributed to renewed Western influence under the Mongol Yuan dynasty. In their determination to extract wealth from China, the Mongols' interest in porcelain was driven by the desire for the profits from trade. Persians dominated the southern sea trade. It was theorized that these merchants provided the impetus behind the appearance of cobalt-decorated porcelain, because the pigment had been used without great success on their own soft pottery during the 12th century. Archeological evidence, on the other hand, has provided Chinese specimens from as early as the 10th–11th century,[1] as well as 13th-century fragments from Jizhou in Jiangxi. It is indisputable, however, that the combination took off during the 14th century. The evolution of the ornament is documented by several important objects: a covered urn dated 1319, two pieces (a funerary urn and granary model) dated 1338, and two temple vases dated 1351.[2]

The white porcelain produced at the Jingdezhen kilns in Jiangxi province proved to be ideally suited to underglaze decoration painted in cobalt blue pigment.[3] Two distinct kinds of porcelains were produced: thickly potted Shufu ware which was covered with a thick opaque white glaze, and the thinly potted Qingbai bluish-white ware.[4] The former seems to have been introduced at the beginning of the Yuan dynasty, as part of experiments with the addition of kaolin that improved the smoothness and the plasticity of the local porcelain stone but also necessitated higher firing temperatures, above 1300 degrees.[5]

This graceful bottle vase, *yuhuchun ping*, is decorated with two phoenixes and a floral scroll in a medium grayish blue; the presence of iron oxides in the cobalt may account for the black blotches. A small amount of naturally occurring iron imparts the bluish-tint to the glaze.

1. A deep bowl from the 10th–11th century with underglaze blue painted decoration was excavated in 1957 from the basement of the Jinsha pagoda in Longquan county, Zhejiang province. Wu Tung and Denise Patry Leidy, "Recent Archaeological Contributions to the Study of Chinese Ceramics," in *Imperial Taste: Chinese Ceramics from the Percival David Foundation* (Los Angeles: Los Angeles County Museum of Art and San Francisco: Chronicle Books, 1989), p. 99.
2. The three earlier pieces—the first in the Jiuzho Provincial Museum, Jiangsu province, and the second two in the Jiangxi Provincial Museum—are illustrated in Wu Tung and Leidy, pp. 99–100; the temple vases in the Percival David Foundation have been widely published.
3. It was painted on the air-dried, absorbent clay surface before the glaze was applied; because the coloring oxide matured at high temperatures, only a single firing was necessary.
4. Shufu is taken from the characters, *shu* and *fu*, translated as "Privy Council," which appear on the objects.
5. Tregear, p. 153.

29

Jiangxi province, Jingdezhen kilns
Ming dynasty, probably Yongle period (1403–1424)

BRUSH WASHER

(early 15th century)
Porcelain with underglaze cobalt decoration
8 1/8 in. diam. (20.7 cm.)
Julius Levy Memorial Fund
BMA 1953.208

Provenance: C. K. Chang, Baltimore

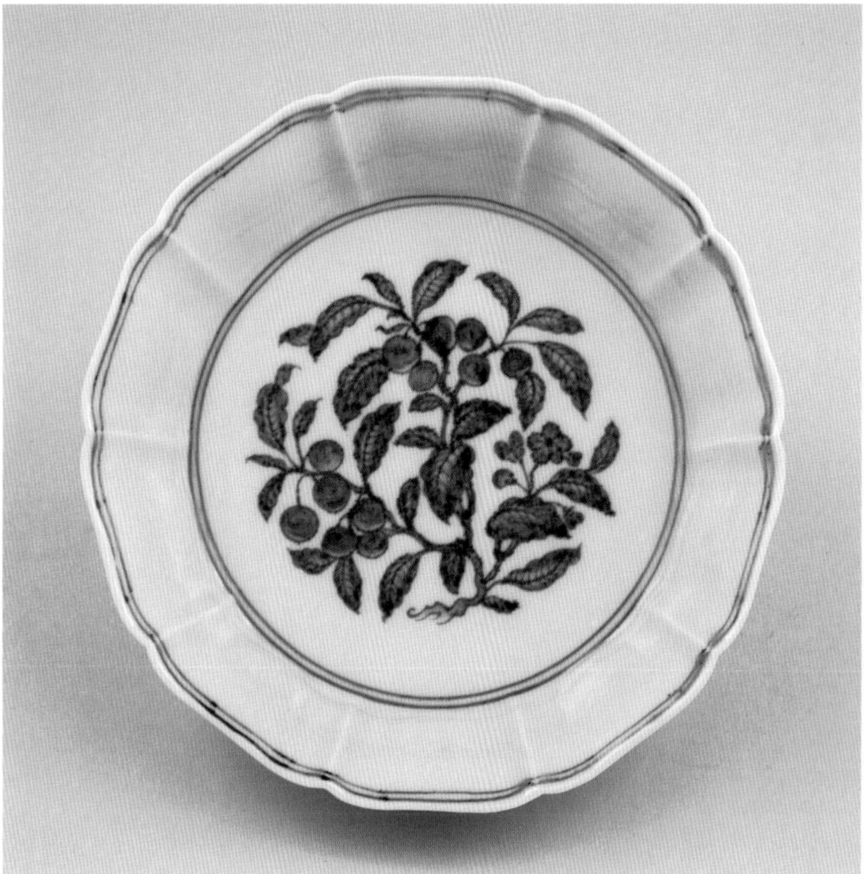

One of the finest pieces in the collection is this foliate-form brush washer. Despite the absence of a reign mark, it nevertheless represents one of the most highly regarded periods in the development of Chinese porcelains. Moreover, both in its materials (the excellence of the porcelain body, the richness of the cobalt pigment) and its design (the scale and balance of the motif executed in strong and lively lines), this object more than merits the esteem generally accorded the fine porcelains of the 15th century.

Superlative examples of 14th-century underglaze cobalt decorated porcelains exist in the numerous large platters exported to the Near East as well as in a pair of large temple jars which are dated to 1351.[1] However, only after the native Chinese dynasty, Ming, was restored in 1368 did a real domestic market develop for this type of decorated porcelain; the kilns responded to the new market with a distinct change in style, one that drew largely upon the Tang dynasty (618–907) for inspiration and that culminated in the wares produced near the end of the Yongle period and during the Xuande period (1426–1435).

Among the most admired products of the Tang were objects made in precious metal. Beautiful, foliate-shaped and decorated gold and silver articles show the direct influence of provincial Persian metalwork. This shape was most widely used in lobed mirrors. Subsequently transmitted from lacquerwares to ceramic forms, foliate motifs were also quickly added to the textile vocabulary.[2]

The brush washer is of a shallow, lobed form. The decoration is restricted to paired thin lines and fruiting sprays. Centered in the interior is a small shrub or branch; its clusters of pendant round fruit and small leaves defy precise botanical identification as the type of elongated leaf is ubiquitous in the genre. Ten quatrefoil medallions around the exterior continue the central motif; within them pairs of peaches alternate with clusters of grapes. The porcelain body is very refined, white, and dense. The glaze is slightly blue, even, and lustrous. Careful preparation of the cobalt pigment is indicated by the depth and intensity of the color although some inexperience is indicated by the "heaped and piled effect," the inky, black splotches resulting from an overconcentration of the pigment.

This object relates directly to a number of marked foliate-shaped bowls, stem cups, and brush washers with similarly organized decoration, more often of dragons rather than fruiting sprays.[3] Characterized by well-balanced and restrained compositions executed with strong and well-controlled lines, porcelain of extremely high quality, and glaze of great beauty, the group epitomizes the finest attributes of Chinese porcelain.

1. These jars are in the Percival David Collection in London.
2. Rawson, p. 125.
3. The fruiting sprays are indicative of the earlier period, as is the absence of a mark; Margaret Medley, in conversation, April 6, 1992.

30

Chinese, Zhejiang province,
Longquan kilns
Ming dynasty (1368–1644)

STORAGE VESSEL (MEIPING)

(1375–1425)
Stoneware with celadon glaze
15 3/8 in. high (39 cm.)
Bequest of Ellen Howard Bayard; Gift of James R. Herbert Boone; Bequest of Eleanor DeForest Boteler; Bequest of Mathilde Whitridge Johnson; Gift of Lawrason Riggs of J; and Gift of William C. Whitridge, Stevenson, Maryland, by exchange
BMA 1989.109

Provenance: J. J. Lally & Co., New York; Private Collection, Japan; Kimura family collection

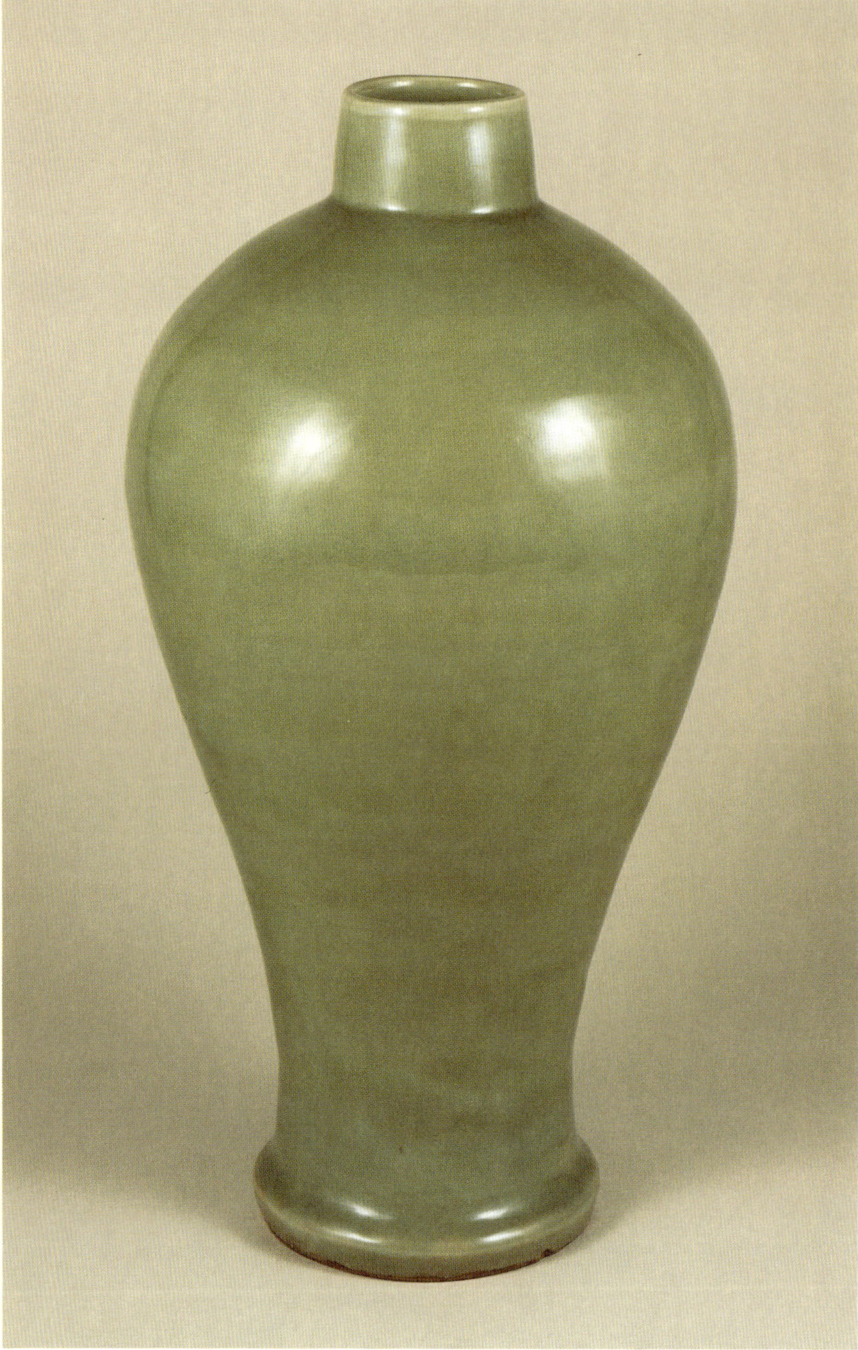

The celadon wares of the enormous kiln complex in southwestern Zhejiang province seem to have mediated between strictly utilitarian wares and refined wares; great quantities, furthermore, were exported to the Near East, southeast Asia, and Japan when these kilns greatly expanded their output during the Yuan dynasty (1271–1368). A frankly voluptuous profile and luminous surface separate this example of later Longquan celadon from much of the material produced during the long decline in the quality of this ware which occurred after the 13th century. The shape, found also in blue-and-white porcelains that most often have lids,[1] displays the bold potting and beautiful proportions that characterize the finest Longquan celadons.[2] Subtle yet distinct color variations exist in the glaze of this striking vessel.[3]

1. A Jun ware example, quite similar to this one, is in the Koger collection; it is attributed to the Yuan dynasty. The blue-and-white vessels are more often assigned to the early Ming.
2. Tregear, p. 167.
3. The greater transparency of the glaze in contrast to the classic Longquan celadons may reflect higher kiln temperatures.

31

Probably Hebei province, Cizhou ware
Ming dynasty (1368–1644)

LARGE STORAGE JAR

(late 15th century)
Stoneware with underglaze iron oxide decoration on white slip
34 1/16 in. high (86.5 cm.)
Gift of Ralph M. Chait
BMA 1929.21.1

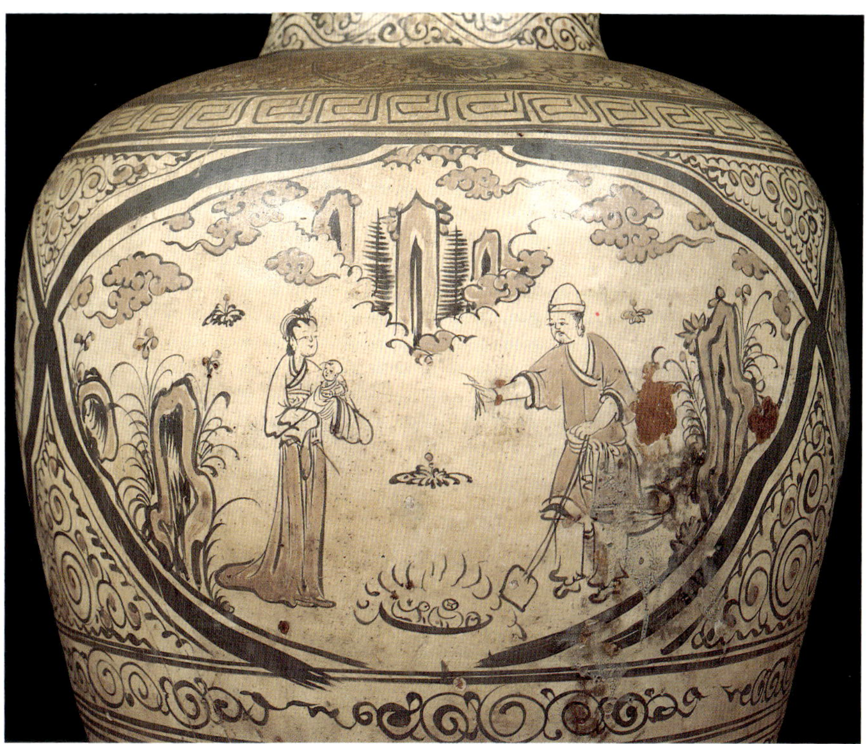

Detail, see p. 6 for full view.

This jar is extraordinary by virtue of its size alone; moreover, it is decorated in an extremely painterly fashion with scenes almost certainly inspired by contemporary fiction. In its type of subject matter, the jar relates to a number of 13th-century Cizhou pillows, the flat surfaces of which provide a more contained and straightforward format in contrast to the broad vertical surface employed here. Parallels in specific elements of its decoration are to be found, however, in late 15th-century blue-and-white porcelains.

Like the smaller Cizhou jar of the preceding century (cat. no. 68), the shape of the vessel is enhanced by the division of the decoration into zones, the central one containing three figural scenes enclosed in loose ogival frames or cartouches.[1] The scenes depict a man looking at a double-gourd container as it falls into a nearby river; another man (who resembles the first) looking over his shoulder at his attendant who carries a bedroll; and a man, attending an open fire, who reaches one hand out to a woman who holds an infant.[2] The first of these (the man with the double-gourd) is found on a pillow ascribed to the 13th century, but the scenes remain otherwise unidentified.[3]

Clues to the dating of this extraordinary vessel are provided by late 15th-century porcelains. The leaf scroll found on the shoulder of the jar bears a marked resemblance to the scroll decorating the body of a large temple vase which is dated 1496.[4] In addition, stiffly rectangular mountains are to be found on both. Similar mountains appear on a late 15th-century *meiping* vase and similar rocks on a dish of the same period.

1. The use of ogival frames is as well a characteristic of a group of 13th-century pillows; see Mino, pp. 138–140.
2. The progression of the scenes is suggested by the fact that there is one figure, then two figures and two distant mountains, and finally three figures and three distant mountains portrayed. Furthermore, it would seem that a journey is involved in the narrative.
3. See Mino, pl. 59, for a pillow in the collection of Mr. and Mrs. Myron Falk, and pp. 140–141 for a reference to the use of adventure stories and supernatural tales.
4. See, for example, Lion-Goldschmidt, nos. 84–88.

32

Possibly Shanxi province, Fahua ware
Ming dynasty (1368–1644)

MEIPING VASE

(c. 1500)
Porcelain with dark blue, turquoise, yellow, and red enamels "on the biscuit"
10 5/8 in. high (27 cm.)
Gift of William C. Whitridge, Stevenson, Maryland
BMA 1979.126

Provenance: William H. Whitridge, Baltimore; Gorer Collection

Published/Exhibited: BMA, *The Whitridge Collection of Chinese Pottery and Porcelain*, June 1–October 15, 1930, p. 61, no. 209, ill.

Fahua wares display an innovative approach to polychrome decoration, in which the different colors are kept separate by thin raised lines. The slip-trailed design was executed before the initial high-temperature firing; low-firing glazes were applied which were fixed by a second firing.[1] Sturdy shapes, bold designs, and certain colors (including dark and light blue, purple, and turquoise with yellow, white, red, and pink used more sparingly) characterize the ware.

This vase is decorated with a standard lotus and water weed motif; in one of the many variations in the standard, there are two lotus blossoms, two leaves, a bud, and an arrowhead or pickerel weed which all spring from cresting waves. The ornate lappets which decorate the shoulder are equally common. The use of outlines trailed in slip, as well as inherently more viscous glazes, accounts for the successful separation of colors which is the essential feature of this distinctive ware.

The term Fahua and its attributed place of origin apparently do not appear in Chinese texts until early in this century.[2] The northern province of Shanxi had in Ming times a long history of producing lead-glazed wares. The popularity of Fahua is suggested by its 16th-century Jingdezhen imitations.

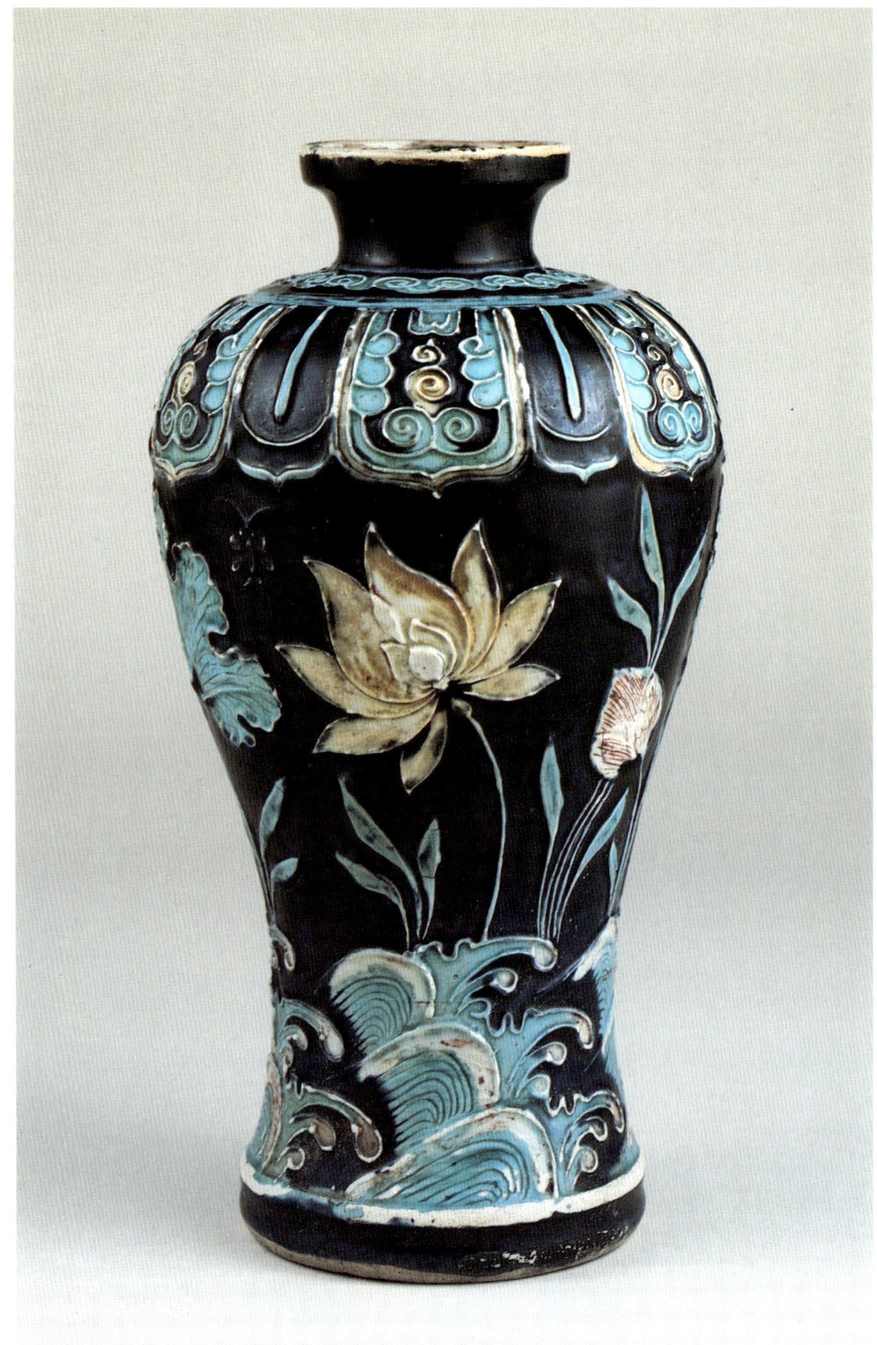

1. That is, a thread of slip (a watered down clay) was trailed over the surface of the vessel, leaving a raised line.
2. *In Pursuit of the Dragon: Traditions and Transitions in Ming Ceramics* (Seattle Art Museum, 1988), p. 122.

33

China, Jiangxi province, Jingdezhen kilns
Ming dynasty, Wanli period (1573–1619)

JAR

Porcelain with green and yellow overglaze lead-silicate enamels
7 1/16 in. high (17.9 cm.)
Period 6-character reign mark within double circle on bottom
Bequest of Blanche Adler
BMA 1941.140

Published/Exhibited: Walters Art Gallery, Baltimore, "Chinese Porcelains," January 18–February 19, 1950.

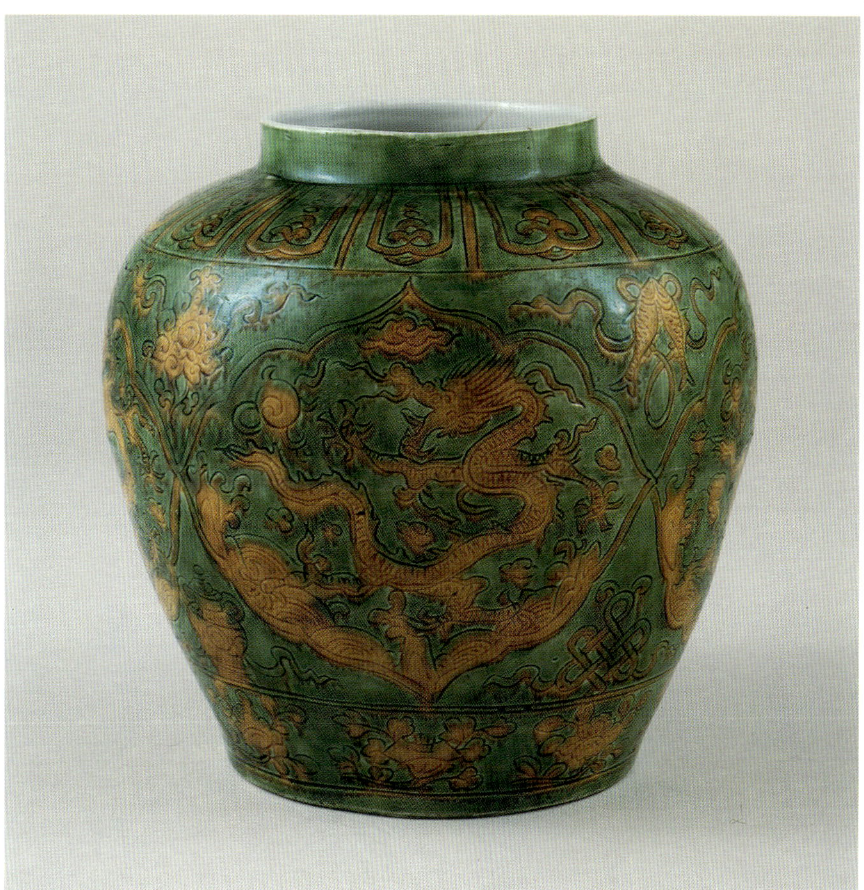

This jar provides an example of yet another decorative technique employed by the artisans of the great Jingdezhen workshops. The design was incised into the body before the jar was covered with a transparent glaze and fired; subsequently, the green and yellow lead-silicate enamels were painted on and the jar was fired again at a much lower temperature. Incised dragon designs covered with green and yellow enamels, known as early as the Yongle period (1403–1425), were very successfully realized during the Zhengde period (1506–1521); interestingly, the colors are reversed on these precursors, with the green dragons placed typically against a yellow ground.[1]

Not at all uncommon, this jar recalls in its shape and decoration several aspects of 14th and 15th-century ceramic repertoire. The very practical *guan* shape is found in Cizhou wares, as well as celadons from Longquan and blue-and-white porcelains from Jingdezhen. Ogival frames and "The Eight Precious Things" also first appear on early porcelains, as do the lappet panels (positioned around the foot, however).

The decoration consists of four quatrefoil cartouches. In each, a writhing dragon, astride waves that surround a central mountain, pursues a ribboned pearl. The color and number of dragons are not without significance. There apparently existed a belief in four dragons which ruled over the four seas encompassing the world. Being at the same time symbolic of the emperor, the dragons are appropriately colored yellow, the emperor's color, the color of the earth, and also the color associated with the fifth of the five directions. In general, yellow symbolized fame, progress, and advancement, and thus would have conveyed an auspicious sentiment in combination with the Eight Precious Things.[2]

1. *Imperial Porcelain of the Yongle and Xuande Periods Excavated from the Site of the Ming Imperial Factory at Jingdezhen* (Hong Kong: Urban Council, 1989), pp. 140–143, nos. 29–30.
2. Eberhard, p. 332.

34

Jiangxi province, Jingdezhen kilns, Wucai ware
Ming dynasty, Wanli period (1573–1619)

FOLIATE-FORM BOX

Porcelain with underglaze cobalt and overglaze enamel decoration
5 1/2 in. diam. (14 cm.)
Period 6-character reign mark within double circle on bottom
Julius Levy Memorial Fund
BMA 1939.253a-b

Provenance: William H. Whitridge, Baltimore

Published/Exhibited: BMA, *The Whitridge Collection of Chinese Pottery and Porcelain*, June 1–October 15, 1930, pp. 45–46, no. 144, ill.; Parke-Bernet, November 16–18, 1939, sale 142, lot 567, ill. p. 121.

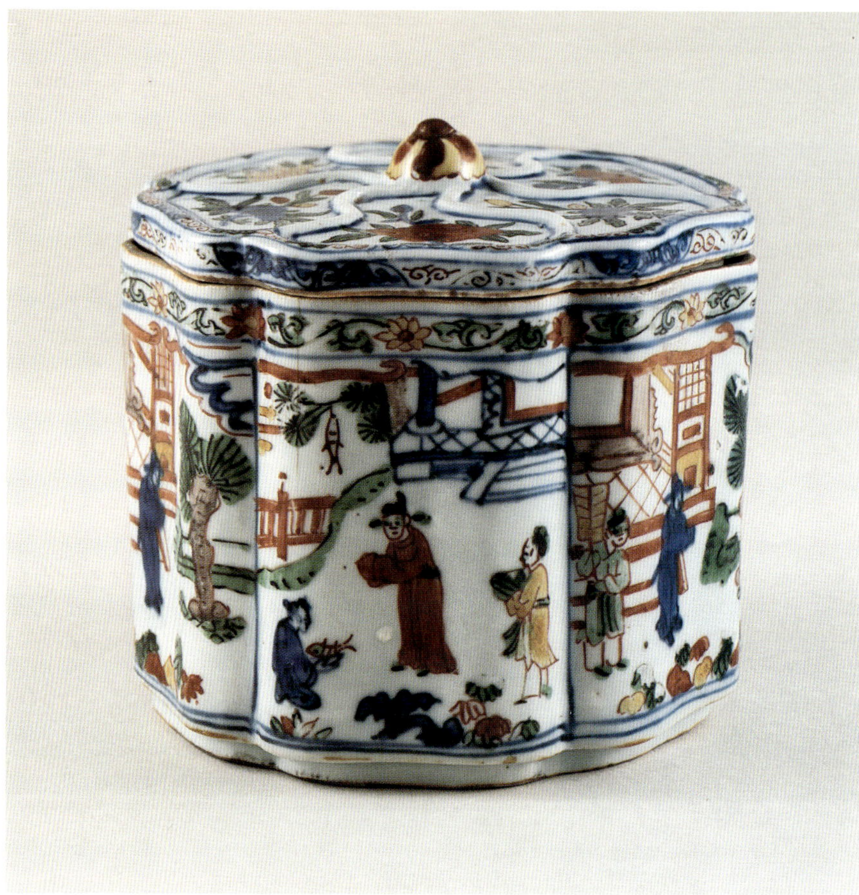

The combination of underglaze cobalt and overglaze polychrome enamel decoration on the porcelain wares of Jingdezhen is associated with two styles, *doucai* (contrasting-colors) and *wucai* (five-colors). The first style may be characterized by the use of underglaze cobalt to outline as well as fill in certain areas of the design, which is then completed by the overglaze application of translucent washes of lead-silicate enamels in soft colors. Documented as early as the Xuande period (1426–1435), the *doucai* style is identified particularly with the extremely delicate and usually small objects from the Chenghua period (1465–1487).[1] The second style, *wucai*, originated during the Jiajing period (1522–1566) and continued into the Kangxi (1662–1722). It is more robust, with overglaze enamel outlines, bold colors, and dark underglaze cobalt in larger and more prominent areas of the design. During the 16th century, especially the later years, the quality of Jingdezhen porcelain declined, largely due to overproduction. Earthquakes and floods damaged the workshops in 1570 and 1571. Court orders for porcelain, however, continued to be enormous—one totaled some 96,000 in 1583—while production for export increased simultaneously.[2]

This box provides a good example of the kind of crowded figural decoration commonly found on Wanli *wucai* porcelain.[3] Typically, limited use is made of underglaze cobalt pigment; on this example, it is restricted to two main figures and line borders around the top and bottom of the side and on the lid. The polychrome lead-silicate enamels that were applied on top of the transparent glaze include red, green, yellow, and brown. Two basic scenes alternate on the six-lobed sides of the box; in all but one, a carp is featured. The motif of the goldfish, popularized during the Jiajing period, is a good-wish pun because the word for fish, *yu*, sounds like the word for wealth or abundance.[4]

1. *Imperial Porcelain of the Yongle and Xuande Periods Excavated from the Site of the Ming Imperial Factory at Jingdezhen* (Hong Kong: Urban Council, 1989), pp. 260–261, no. 89.
2. Lion-Goldschmidt, p. 182.
3. The box was molded, decorated with cobalt pigment, glazed, and fired at a high temperature. The enamels were added then, and it was fired a second time at a much lower temperature.
4. For example, the scene of a fisherman selling carp is a rebus for "he hopes for a good income and social advancement." Eberhard, p. 107.

35

Jiangxi province, Jingdezhen kilns
Ming dynasty, Wanli period
(1573–1619)

VASE WITH DRAGON HANDLES

Porcelain with bright green enamel glaze and residue of overglaze gilt decoration
17 13/16 in. high (45.2 cm.)
Wanli 6-character reign mark on rim
Julius Levy Memorial Fund
BMA 1939.248

Provenance: William H. Whitridge, Baltimore; Duveen Brothers, New York; J. Pierpont Morgan, New York; Marsden J. Perry, Providence, Rhode Island; William Arkwright, Esq., Chesterfield, England

Published/Exhibited: BMA, *The Whitridge Collection of Chinese Pottery and Porcelain*, June 1–October 15, 1930, p. 84, no. 313, ill.; Parke-Bernet, New York, November 16–18, 1939, sale 142, no. 487, ill. p. 98; Walters Art Gallery, "Chinese Porcelains," January 18–February 19, 1950; BMA, *A Picture Book*, 1955, ill. p. 90; Walters Art Gallery, "Chinese Ceramics," April 30–September 15, 1956; Kent Roberts Greenfield, "The Museum: Its First Half Century," *Annual I*, BMA, 1966, ill. p. 29.

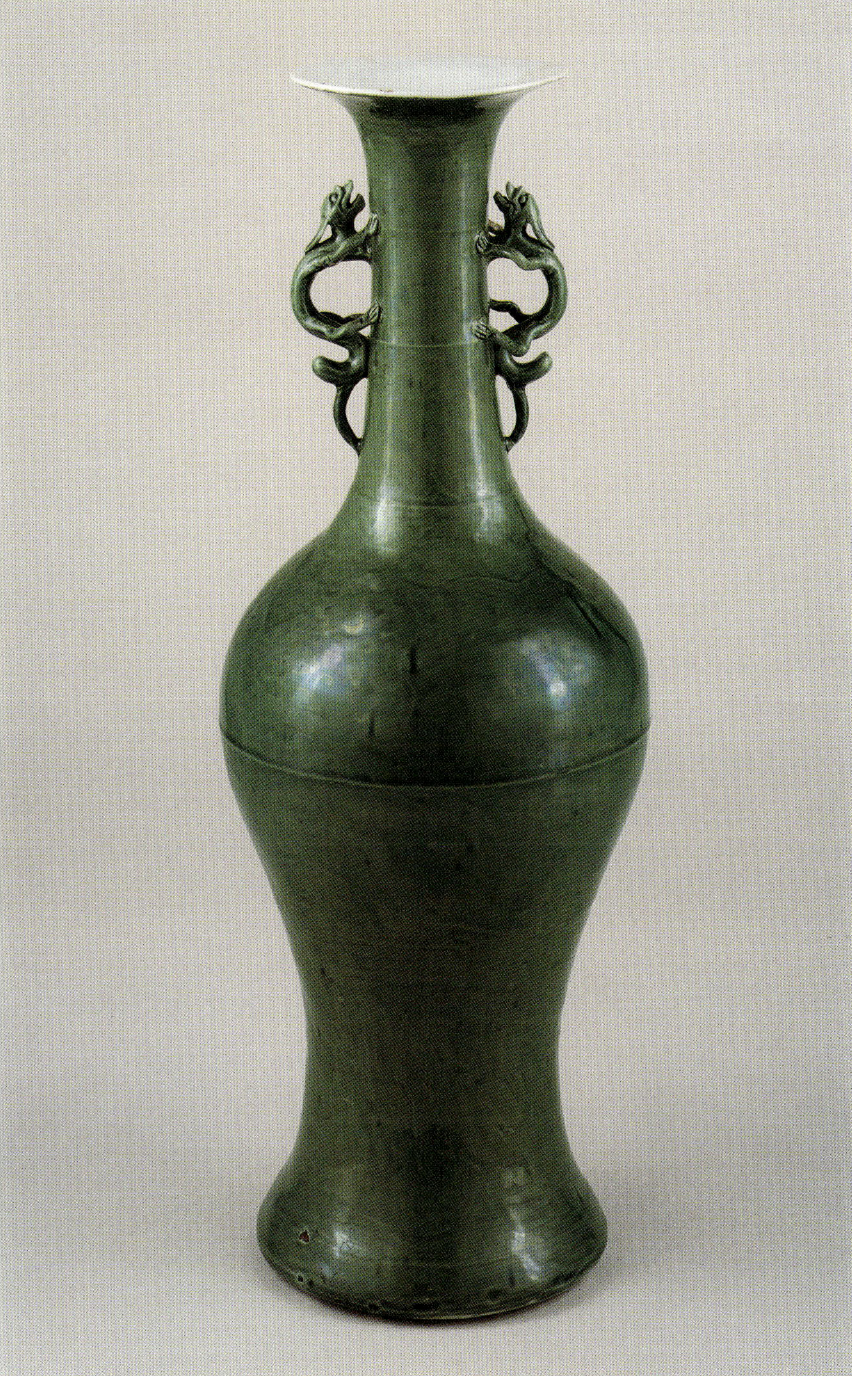

There are strong parallels between this vase and mid-16th-century wares; specifically, the use of dense overglaze gilt decoration, termed "gold-brocaded" (*kinrande*) by the Japanese, as well as the monochrome green lead glaze which first appeared at that time. This bright, strong green glaze is a rarity, though Kangxi (1662–1722) examples of the color do exist as do a few from the Shunzhi period (1644–1661). By the later Wanli, increasingly complicated shapes were ordered from the Jingdezhen kilns. The exaggerated, reverse curves that distinguish this vessel are very much in keeping with that period.

The combination of the dragon motif and the color green is most appropriate because the green dragon of the east is one of the four animals traditionally associated with the cardinal directions. The vase was decorated originally with an overglaze gilt floral motif. An oily residue of the adhesive which affixed the gold to the surface remains to document the flowers, leaves, butterflies, and dragonflies as well as scrolls, bands, and diaper patterns. The vase was constructed of seven sections, the seams of which are plainly visible. The rounded foot rim was trimmed with a knife; the recessed foot cavity is unevenly glazed.

There is a smaller, but otherwise identical, vase in the Widener Collection at the National Gallery of Art (C-385); it also was in the Morgan Collection.

36

Jiangxi province, Jingdezhen kilns
Qing dynasty, Kangxi period
(1662–1722)

VASE

(c. 1683–1710)
Porcelain with underglaze cobalt decoration, silver collar
10 in. high (25.4 cm.)
Bequest of Francis Burns Harvey
BMA 1931.20.90

During the late 17th and 18th century great proficiency was attained by craftsmen of the porcelain city, Jingdezhen, in the production of enormous quantities of underglaze cobalt decorated wares, which were used within China as well as exported especially to Europe. The refinement of the various constituent clays of porcelain as well as the transparent glaze, along with the cobalt oxide, resulted in the brilliance characteristic of wares dating to the Kangxi period.

This baluster vase is decorated with a scene rendered in penciled outlines filled with washes ranging in color from light blue to sapphire blue. It shows four figures in an interior. A handsome young scholar or official is seated behind a table and before him is seated a beautiful young woman who looks over her shoulder away from him. At the far left an old woman and an old, bearded man observe the central action. Identification of the scene with a literary source has proved impossible, although "there can be no doubt of the ultimate primacy of woodblock prints as the original source of much, if not most, of the Qing repertoire of figurative painting."[1] The remaining space contains a banana or plantain tree, rock, balustrade, and full moon.

1. Craig Clunas, "The West Chamber: A Literary Theme in Chinese Porcelain Decoration," *Transactions of the Oriental Ceramic Society*, London, 1983, p. 75.

37

Fujian province, Dehua kilns
Qing dynasty, Kangxi period
(1662–1722)

GUANYIN

(c. 1660–1690)
Porcelain with transparent glaze
17 3/8 in. high (44.2 cm.)
Seal mark on back: Shanren Huijiang
Bequest of Eleanor M. Lehr
BMA 1964.43.1

Some 250 miles to the south and east of Jingdezhen, another type of fine porcelain was produced at the Dehua kilns of Fujian province. It was composed almost entirely of an excellent local porcelain stone and fired at temperatures in excess of 1400 degrees in beehive-shaped, multichambered kilns.[1] The nearly complete fusion of glaze and clay body accounts for the thick, lustrous glaze. Although rather inferior blue-and-white, as well as monochrome porcelains were produced, Dehua is famous for this beautiful white porcelain which was made from the late Ming dynasty on; "tens of Ming dynasty kilns have been discovered at Dehua, but more than a hundred Qing sites are known."[2] Dating is difficult because both the materials and the shapes have remained relatively unchanged; from dated examples, it is evident that early works have a certain warmth of tone and heaviness absent in 18th-century and later objects. Popular with the late Ming literati and exported in great numbers, this porcelain seems to have gone strangely unnoticed by the court.

Dehua porcelain was put to the best use possible as demonstrated by its characteristic shapes. Its color seems especially appropriate for archaistic ritual vessels, while the many devotional figures attest to the plasticity of this unique porcelain stone. The most frequently encountered figures are those of the Buddha and Guanyin.

Guanyin, the Goddess of Mercy, was extremely popular in China, though more in the south than the north. Being a Bodhisattva, she had attained enlightenment and was thus able to enter Nirvana; she chose, however, to remain in this world to aid the rest of humankind in its struggle to escape the cycle of rebirth as she herself had done. People prayed to her for the birth of sons and for wealth, among other things. The potter, ostensibly Huijiang, has followed convention by indicating her privileged past through her flowing robe and elongated earlobes, her association with Buddha by her crown, and her masculine origin in the Indian Avalokitesvara, God of Compassion, by her bare foot.[3] Supremely compassionate yet completely indifferent to the endless sorrows she hears, this Guanyin is pure and serene, qualities epitomized by the porcelain of Dehua.

1. The stone consists primarily of quartz derived from decomposed granite which when crushed and washed can be used alone to make porcelain.
2. S. J. Vainker, *Chinese Pottery and Porcelain: From Prehistory to the Present* (New York: George Braziller, Inc., 1991), p. 170.
3. P. J. Donnelly, *Blanc de Chine: The Porcelain of Tehua in Fukien* (New York: Frederick A. Praeger, Inc., 1969), p. 359, identifies the mark and discusses this fancy name, p. 283.

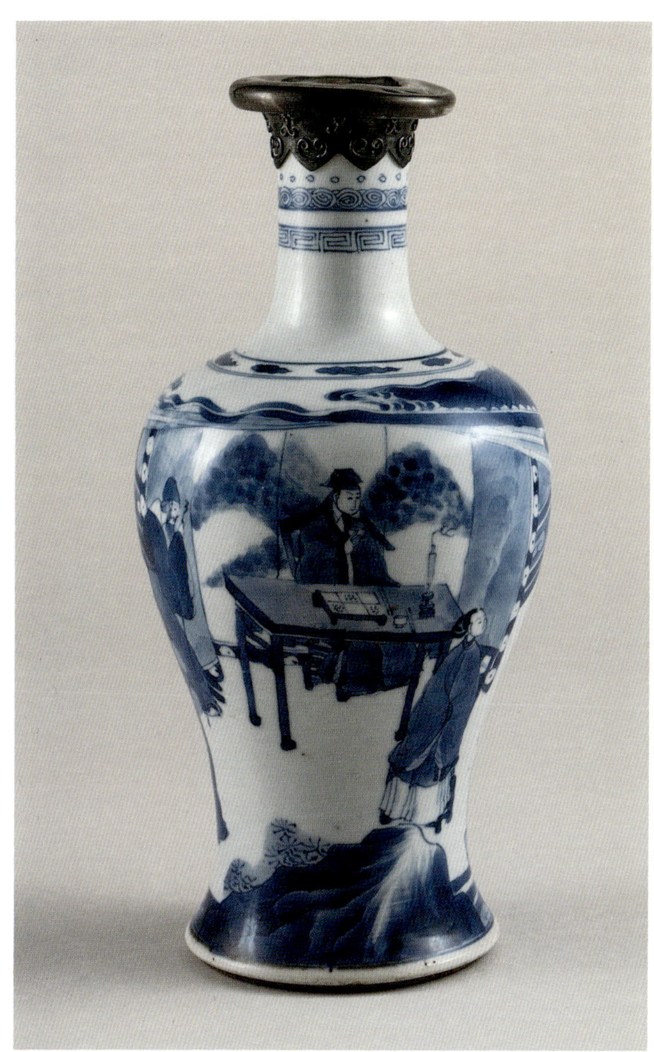

36

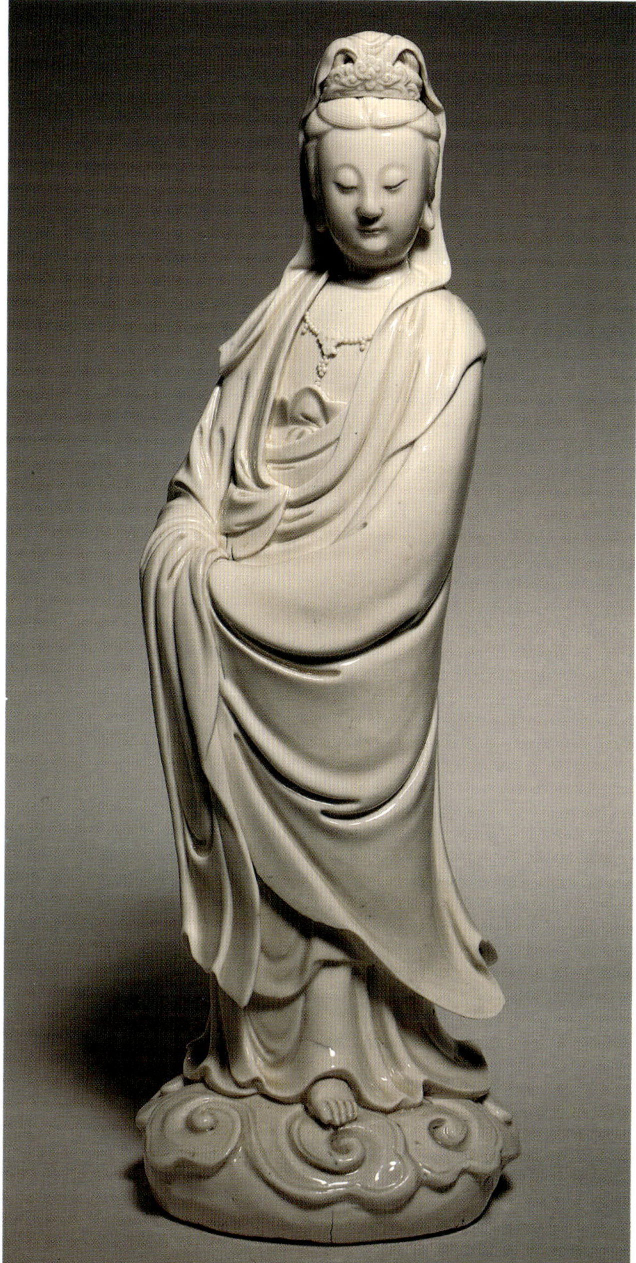

37

38

Jiangxi province, Jingdezhen kilns
Qing dynasty, Kangxi period
(1662–1722)

ZUN-SHAPED VASE

(late 17th century)
Porcelain with imitation Song dynasty Longquan-type celadon glaze
15 13/16 in. high (40.1 cm.)
Spurious 6-character Chenghua reign mark on bottom
Frank J. and Elizabeth L. Goodnow Collection
BMA 1942.70.413

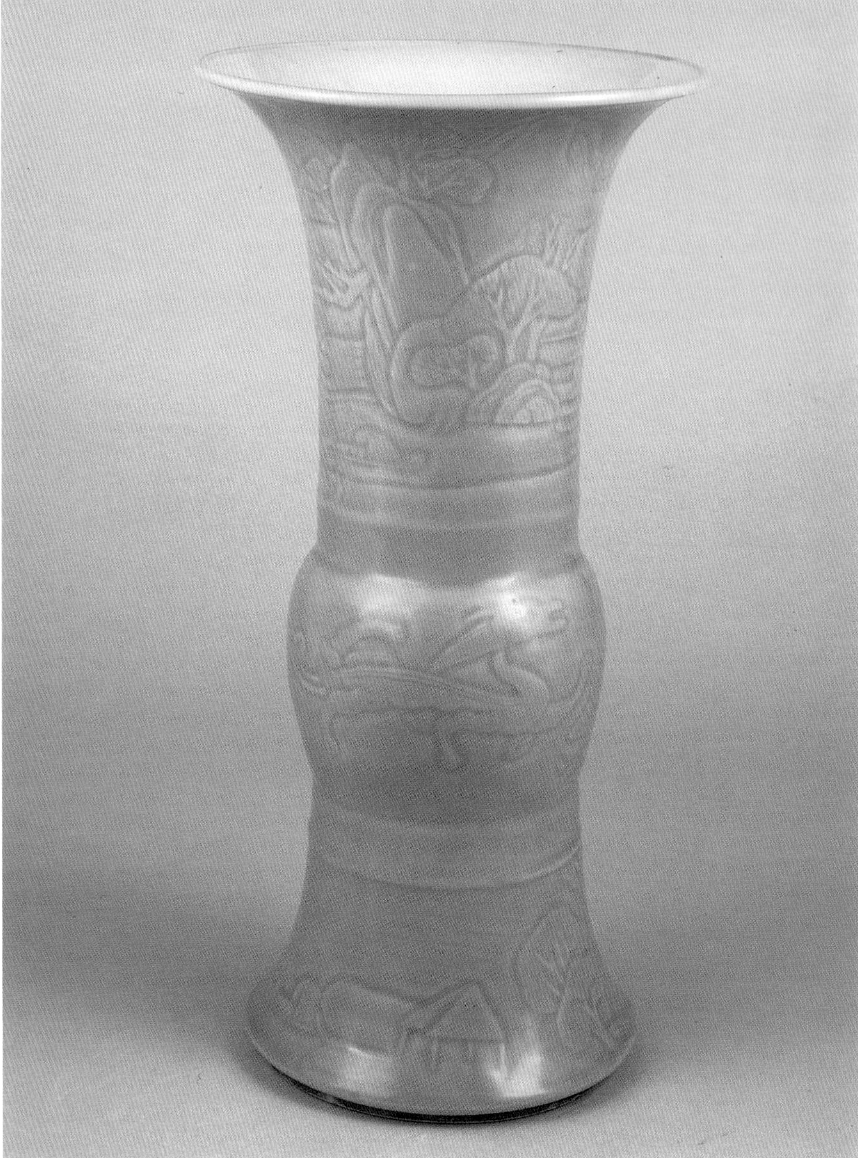

This vase provides an early example of archaistic sensibility that became extremely fashionable later in the 18th century. Its shape is based on a ritual bronze form, the *zun*, popular from the 13th to the 10th century B.C., while its glaze and decoration derive from wares produced particularly during the 13th and 14th centuries at Longquan kilns. This debt to the past is trumpeted by the 6-character Chenghua reign mark (1465–1487), whereby respect is accorded the porcelains of the earlier Ming period. It is, however, impossible to find any direct correspondence between the small, delicately painted porcelains of the late 15th century and this imposing late 17th-century vase.

The Longquan kilns of Zhejiang province, particularly from the 12th to the 15th centuries, produced vast quantities of green-glazed stonewares. Many large dishes made during the late 14th and early 15th century display carved decoration in bold floral motifs. This vase is made of porcelain obtained from finer white clays fired to a much higher temperature; the celadon glaze may not vary greatly from that used at Longquan but, because of the change in body composition, the appearance is vastly different.[1] The bright, pale green color is used to advantage with the dense molded and carved decoration.

The Southern Song (1127–1279) was another time in which ancient bronze forms inspired ceramics, but in a stricter way. One example from the 13th century is a particularly faithful copy of the *gu* or *zun* form, in contrast to which this is a far more stylized interpretation.[2] The shape lends itself to three distinct zones of decoration that on the bronze original were generally filled with patterns assumed to have significant ritual symbolism: monster masks (*taotie*), confronted dragons and birds, cicada. The molded and carved decoration considered here, however, owes more to the secular landscapes which were standard for underglaze-cobalt painted porcelains from the same period. The ancient dragon motif, reinterpreted here with the dragons in sequence, is retained on the central register however. The top and bottom sections contain landscapes dense with mountains, trees, buildings and figures, rivers, and fishermen in boats. Spatial considerations are treated less successfully than on painted wares where gradations of color permit a greater distinction between near and far distances.

1. *Iron in the Fire*, p. 76, no. 82.
2. *Imperial Taste: Chinese Ceramics from the Percival David Foundation* (Los Angeles: Los Angeles County Museum of Art and San Francisco: Chronicle Books, 1989), p. 46, no. 21.

39

Jiangxi province, Jingdezhen kilns
Qing dynasty, Yongzheng period (1723–1735)

VASE

Porcelain with imitation Song dynasty Guan-type glaze
10 7/16 in. high (26.5 cm.)
Period 6-character seal script mark on bottom
Frank J. and Elizabeth L. Goodnow Collection
BMA 1942.70.343

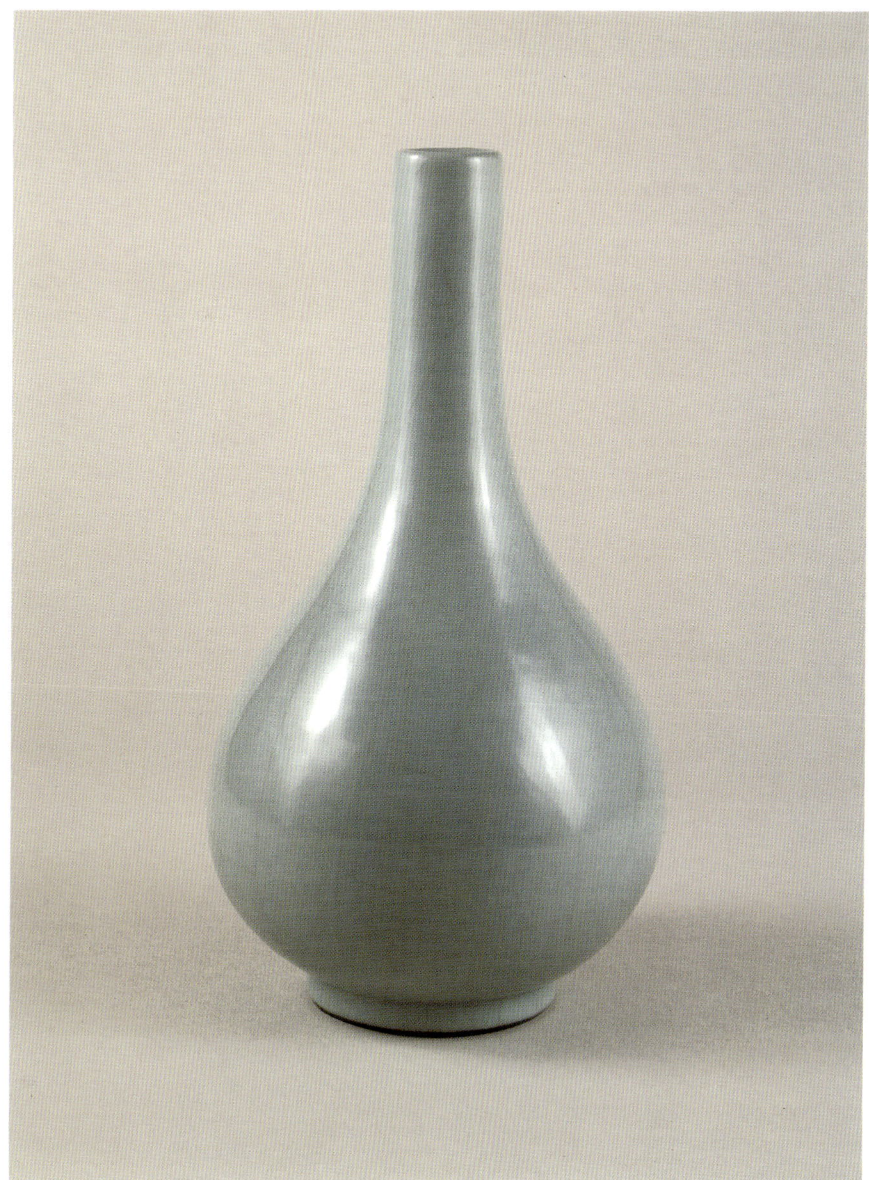

Song dynasty *guan*-ware glazes were widely copied in the 18th century but rarely as successfully as on this lovely vase. The soft watery green glaze is crackled like its 12th-century prototype, and its unglazed foot rim is stained brown as well. The crackles were obtained by multiple glaze layers together with manipulation of the kiln temperature. Strong diagonals, which result from tension that remains in the thrown form twisting the crackle, accentuate both the rounded body and the long tapered neck.[1] Not only the shape but also the beauty of the glaze are enhanced by these widely-spaced crackles because they catch light, thereby creating both the luminous surface and mesmerizing illusion of depth.

1. For an explanation of the connection between pieces thrown on the potter's wheel and the diagonal patterns of crackle, see Tregear, p. 132.

40
Gansu province, Yangshao culture, Banshan phase
Neolithic period
JAR
(c. 2500 B.C.)
Earthenware with black and red pigments
8 7/8 in. diam. (22.5 cm.)
Julius Levy Memorial Fund
BMA 1939.251
Provenance: William H. Whitridge, Baltimore; Ralph M. Chait, New York

41
Shang dynasty (c. 16th–11th century B.C.)
TRIPOD VESSEL (LI)
Unglazed earthenware, cord-marked
8 1/16 in. high (20.5 cm.)
Julius Levy Memorial Fund
BMA 1939.250
Provenance: William H. Whitridge, Baltimore

42
Western Han period (206 B.C.–A.D. 8)
COCOON-FORM JAR WITH ABSTRACTED FELINE DECORATION
(2nd century B.C.)
Gray earthenware with turquoise, white, pink, dark red, orange, and black pigments
10 3/4 in. wide (27.4 cm.)
Purchase with exchange funds from Julius Levy Memorial Fund
BMA 1992.212
Provenance: Andrew Kahane, Limited, New York

43
Han dynasty (206 B.C.–A.D. 220)
WINE STORAGE VESSEL (HU)
Earthenware with red, pink, white, orange, blue, and black pigments
13 1/4 in. high (33.6 cm.)
Gift of Howard C. Hollis, by exchange
BMA 1990.57
Provenance: J.J. Lally & Co., New York

44
Eastern Han period (25–220)
HILL JAR
Description: hunt scene frieze on side of jar; bear-form tripod legs; lid in the form of a mountain
Earthenware with degraded green lead-fluxed glaze
7 3/4 in. diam. (19.7 cm.)
Frank J. and Elizabeth L. Goodnow Collection
BMA 1942.70.244a-b

45
Eastern Han period (25–220)
COVERED TRIPOD (DING)
Description: elephant-head legs
Earthenware with degraded green lead-fluxed glaze
10 11/16 in. wide (27.2 cm.)
Julius Levy Memorial Fund
BMA 1939.239a-b
Provenance: William H. Whitridge, Baltimore

46
Eastern Han period (25–220)
BOWL
Description: dragon-head handle
Earthenware with green lead-fluxed glaze
8 15/16 in. wide (22.7 cm.)
Julius Levy Memorial Fund
BMA 1939.240
Provenance: William H. Whitridge, Baltimore; Hart Collection, Shanghai

47
Eastern Han period (25–220)
SHALLOW DISH
Earthenware with green lead-fluxed glaze
8 1/16 in. diam. (20.5 cm.)
Julius Levy Memorial Fund
BMA 1939.241
Provenance: William H. Whitridge, Baltimore; Hart Collection, Shanghai

48
Eastern Han period (25–220)
LADLE
Earthenware with green lead-fluxed glaze
5 in. long (12.7 cm.)
Gift of Lawrason Riggs of J
BMA 1945.59.13.1

49
Eastern Han period (25–220)
FIGURE OF A DIGNITARY
(2nd century)
Earthenware with green lead-fluxed glaze
17 in. high (43.1 cm.)
Purchase with exchange funds from Gift of Harry Nail; Bequest of Caecilia H. Norton; Gift of Mr. and Mrs. William B. Oliver; Gift of Ruth Frank Ring, Cockeysville, Maryland; and Gift of Mrs. Mason Knox, from the Estate of Julia Rogers
BMA 1990.120
Provenance: C. C. Wang, New York; Countess Cigogna, London

50
Zhejiang province, Yue ware
Eastern Jin dynasty (317–420)
GROUP OF FARM ANIMALS
(4th century)
Description: .28) dog reclining in circular dish; .29) pair of birds in open-work coop; .30) pig in round pen with vertical slats
Stoneware with gray-green glaze
.28) 5 1/16 in. diam. (12.9 cm.);
.29) 5 11/16 in. wide (14.5 cm.);
.30) 5 7/8 in. diam. (15 cm.)
Purchase with exchange funds from Julius Levy Memorial Fund; Gift of Cornelius Ruxton Love, Jr.; Gift of Capt. Israel N. Munaker; Gift of J. Gilman D'Arcy Paul; Bequest of John Henry Scarff; and Gift of Alan Wurtzburger
BMA 1991.28-30
Provenance: J. J. Lally & Co., New York

51
Probably Henan province
Northern Wei dynasty (386–535)
FIGURE OF A COURT LADY
(early 6th century)
Gray earthenware with red, black, white, and pink pigments, encrustation, and dirt
14 7/8 in. high (37.7 cm.)
Purchase with exchange funds from Frank J. and Elizabeth L. Goodnow Collection
BMA 1990.121
Provenance: C. C. Wang, New York

52
Possibly Northern Qi (550–577)
TOMB GUARDIAN (ZHENMU SHOU)
Description: dog's paws, trefoil tail, anthropomorphized face with leonine features, scaly scalp, and horns
Red earthenware with traces of slip and pigment, encrustation
12 13/16 in. high (32.5 cm.)
Gift of Terri and Erwin Harris, Baltimore
BMA 1990.304

53
Tang dynasty (618–907)
AMPHORA VASE
(early 7th century)
Description: dragon handles at neck
White earthenware with degraded straw-colored lead-fluxed glaze over white slip
12 7/16 in. high (31.6 cm.)
Gift of Douglas Wise de Richelieu
BMA 1958.60

54
Tang dynasty (618–907)
PAIR OF OXEN
(7th century)
White earthenware with traces of black and orange pigment
.1) 10 1/4 in. long (26 cm.);
.2) 9 7/16 in. long (24 cm.)
Gift of David K. E. Bruce
BMA 1956.149.1-2

55
Probably Henan or Shaanxi province
Tang dynasty (618–907)
FIGURE OF A TOCHARIAN GROOM
(7th century)
Description: standing with feet and legs together, arms close to body, head bent slightly; wearing long head scarf and loose, belted garment
Buff earthenware with straw lead-fluxed glaze
11 1/8 in. high (28.2 cm.)
Gift of Terri and Erwin Harris, Baltimore
BMA 1990.305

56
Possibly Henan province
Tang dynasty (618–907)
SMALL BOWL
(8th century)
Description: molded decoration in Sassanian motif
Earthenware with green, amber, and transparent lead-fluxed glazes
3 7/8 in. diam. (9.8 cm.)
Gift of Lawrason Riggs of J
BMA 1945.59.22
Provenance: Ralph M. Chait, New York

57
Possibly Henan province
Tang dynasty (618–907)
SMALL BOWL
(8th century)
Description: molded decoration in Sassanian motif
Earthenware with green, amber, and transparent lead-fluxed glazes
3 15/16 in. diam. (10 cm.)
Gift of Lawrason Riggs of J
BMA 1945.59.23
Provenance: Ralph M. Chait, New York

58
Shaanxi or Henan province
Tang dynasty (618–907)
WATER DROPPER IN THE FORM OF A SHELL
(8th century)
White earthenware with green, blue, and amber lead-fluxed glazes
4 3/8 in. long (11.2 cm.)
Purchase with exchange funds from the Julius Levy Memorial Fund
BMA 1991.91

59
Henan or Shaanxi province
Tang dynasty (618–907)
EARTH SPIRIT (QITOU)
(700–750)
Description: horned and winged lion crouching on a rock
Earthenware with green, amber, and transparent lead-fluxed glazes
27 1/16 in. high (68.8 cm.)
Gift of Terri and Erwin Harris, Baltimore
BMA 1985.290

60
Tang dynasty (618–907)
HORSE- AND MONKEY-HEADED FIGURES
(8th–9th century)
Description: two of the twelve Earthly Branches (Shengxiao) of the Chinese Duodenary Calendar
Red earthenware with slip and traces of pigment
.1) 7 1/4 in. high (18.5 cm.);
.2) 7 3/8 in. high (18.8 cm.)
Gift of Terri and Erwin Harris, Baltimore
BMA 1986.192.1-2

61
Tang dynasty (618–907)
(CHILD'S) PILLOW
(9th century)
Description: rectangular, with upturned ends
Marbled white and brown clays over coarse clay core, with yellow lead glaze
5 1/8 in. long (13 cm.)
Gift of Saidie A. May, by exchange
BMA 1988.650
Provenance: J. J. Lally & Co., New York; Rudolph Schaeffer, San Francisco

62
Hebei province, Cizhou kilns
Northern Song period (960–1127)
LOBED BOWL
(10th–11th century)
Stoneware with clear glaze over white slip
4 13/16 in. diam. (12.2 cm.)
Julius Levy Memorial Fund
BMA 1939.244.1
Provenance: William H. Whitridge, Baltimore

63
Hebei province, Cizhou kilns
Northern Song period (960–1127)
LAMP
(10th–11th century)
Stoneware with clear glaze over white slip
6 1/8 in. diam. (15.5 cm.)
Julius Levy Memorial Fund
BMA 1939.244.2
Provenance: William H. Whitridge, Baltimore

64
Henan or Hebei province, Cizhou ware
Southern Song period (1127–1279)
CONICAL TEA BOWL
(12th century)
Description: matte reddish-brown glaze on exterior
Stoneware with black and brown glazes
6 5/16 in. diam. (16 cm.)
Julius Levy Memorial Fund
BMA 1957.76
Provenance: Howard C. Hollis, Cleveland

65
Fujian province, Jian ware
Southern Song period (1127–1279)
TEA BOWL
Stoneware with hare's fur glaze
4 13/16 in. diam. (12.2 cm.)
Gift of Lawrason Riggs of J
BMA 1945.59.12

66
Fujian province, Jian ware
Southern Song period (1127–1279)
TEA BOWL
Stoneware with streaked brown glazes
4 7/8 in. diam. (12.3 cm.)
Julius Levy Memorial Fund
BMA 1959.46
Provenance: Howard C. Hollis, Cleveland

67
Jiangxi province, Jizhou ware
Southern Song period (1127–1279)
TEA BOWL WITH PAPER-RESIST DECORATION OF PLUM BLOSSOMS
Description: scattered florets on interior
Stoneware with brown dressing under mottled brown glaze
4 $^{5}/_{8}$ in. diam. (11.7 cm.)
Gift of J. Gilman D'Arcy Paul, by exchange
BMA 1988.648
Provenance: Eskenazi Limited, London

68
Probably Hebei province, Cizhou ware
Yuan dynasty (1271–1368)
JAR
(14th century)
Description: seated woman holding lotus; scholar beneath plum tree beside river; lotus blossom; each within cartouche
Stoneware with underglaze iron oxide decoration on white slip
11 $^{9}/_{16}$ in. high (29.3 cm.)
Gift of Saidie A. May
BMA 1940.39

69
Fujian province, Dehua ware
Yuan dynasty (1271–1368)
SHALLOW BOWL
(14th century)
Description: impressed lotus leaves on exterior
Porcelain with transparent glaze
8 in. diam. (20.3 cm.)
Gift of Jennis Roy Galloway
BMA 1971.6.1
Provenance: Frank Caro, New York

70
Jiangxi province, Jingdezhen kilns
Yuan dynasty (1271–1368)
ROUND COVERED BOX
(14th century)
Porcelain with grayish blue-white glaze decorated with iron-brown spots
3 $^{1}/_{8}$ in. diam. (8 cm.)
Gift of Terri and Erwin Harris, Baltimore
BMA 1991.218a-b

71
Zhejiang province, Longquan kilns
Yuan dynasty (1271–1368)
SMALL PEAR-SHAPED VASE
(14th century)
Stoneware with celadon glaze
6 $^{1}/_{2}$ in. high (16.5 cm.)
Julius Levy Memorial Fund
BMA 1988.66
Provenance: J. J. Lally & Co., New York

72
Zhejiang province, Longquan kilns
Yuan dynasty (1271–1368)
DISH
(14th century)
Description: molded fish in interior
Stoneware with celadon glaze
8 $^{3}/_{4}$ in. diam. (22.3 cm.)
Gift of Jennis Roy Galloway
BMA 1970.25.1

73
Zhejiang province, Longquan kilns
Ming dynasty (1368–1644)
LARGE DISH
(15th century)
Description: loose foliate scroll around lip and lotus blossom in well
Stoneware with celadon glaze
14 $^{7}/_{8}$ in. diam. (37.8 cm.)
Gift of Jennis Roy Galloway
BMA 1971.6.2

74
Jiangxi province, Jingdezhen kilns
Ming dynasty, probably Yongle period (1403–1424)
BOWL
(early 15th century)
Description: finely painted flower blossoms and fruiting spray on interior
Porcelain with underglaze cobalt decoration
8 $^{5}/_{16}$ in. diam. (21.1 cm.)
Julius Levy Memorial Fund
BMA 1953.207
Provenance: C. K. Chang, Baltimore

75
Possibly Shanxi or Hebei province, Cizhou ware
Ming dynasty (1368–1644)
BOTTLE (MEIPING)
(15th century)
Description: three cartouches of dancing boy, bird, and chrysanthemum
Stoneware with iron oxide decoration on white slip, under turquoise glaze
10 $^{1}/_{8}$ in. high (25.7 cm.)
Gift of Terri and Erwin Harris, Baltimore
BMA 1988.1432

76
Shaanxi province, Fahua ware
Ming dynasty (1368–1644)
PAIR OF VASES
(c. 1500)
Description: peacock, crane, peony flowers, and rocks
Porcelain decorated with purplish-blue, pink, yellow, and turquoise enamels
.1) 13 $^{1}/_{2}$ in. high (34.3 cm.);
.2) 13 in. high (33 cm.)
The Mary Frick Jacobs Collection
BMA 1940.150.1-2

77
Jiangxi province, Jingdezhen kilns
Ming dynasty, Jiajing period (1522–1566)
LARGE BOTTLE VASE (YUHUCHUNPING)
Description: lotus flowers and vines
Porcelain with underglaze cobalt decoration
Period 6-character reign mark within double circle on bottom
12 $^{1}/_{2}$ in. high (31.8 cm.)
Gift of Fred J. van Slyke
BMA 1965.41.1

78
Jiangxi province
Ming dynasty (1368–1644)
PAIR OF ATTENDANTS
(c. late 16th century)
Description: the male carries a rectangular box; the female, a basin
Earthenware with white slip, green and amber lead-fluxed glazes, and white, black, and red pigments
.1) 19 $^{5}/_{16}$ in. high (49 cm.);
.2) 19 $^{1}/_{2}$ in. high (49.5 cm.)
Purchase with exchange funds from Gift of David K. E. Bruce, in Memory of Mrs. Dwight F. Davis; Gift of Ralph M. Chait; Gift of Stanford Cohan; Gift of Jennis Roy Galloway; Gift of Mrs. Mason Knox, from the Estate of Julia Rogers; Gift of Randolph Mordecai; Gift from the Estate of Ruth Marshall Mugford; and Gift of Mark T. Benson
BMA 1991.32.1-2
Provenance: J. J. Lally & Co., New York

79
Fujian province
Ming dynasty (1368–1644)
BOWL
(late 16th century)
Description: stamped, stylized shou characters and elaborate covered vases
Porcelain with underglaze (gray-blue) cobalt decoration
9 11/16 in. diam. (24.6 cm.)
Gift of Mr. and Mrs. R. Austin Tydings
BMA 1978.87

80
Jiangxi province, Jingdezhen kilns
Ming dynasty, Wanli period (1573–1619)
ROUGE BOX
Description: small applied branch on lid
Porcelain with underglaze cobalt decoration
1 13/16 in. diam. (4.7 cm.)
Bequest of Mathilde Whitridge Johnson
BMA 1976.95.16a-b
Provenance: William H. Whitridge, Baltimore; Captain F. Brinkley Collection

81
Jiangxi province, Jingdezhen kilns
Ming dynasty (1368–1644)
KENDI
(c. 1620)
Description: five panels of flowers alternating with leaves; spirals surrounded by dots around spout and shoulder
Porcelain with underglaze cobalt decoration
7 13/16 in. high (19.8 cm.)
Gift of Mrs. Mason Knox, from the Estate of Julia Rogers
BMA 1945.22.2

82
Jiangxi province, Jingdezhen kilns
Ming dynasty, Wanli period (1573–1619)
BOTTLE VASE
(c. 1620)
Description: six panels of flowers and rocks alternating with beribboned double-gourds
Porcelain with underglaze cobalt decoration
10 1/4 in. high (26.1 cm.)
Gift of Mrs. Mason Knox, from the Estate of Julia Rogers
BMA 1945.22.3

83
Jiangxi province, Jingdezhen kilns
Ming dynasty, Wanli period (1573–1619)
DISH
(early 17th century)
Description: shells, books, fans, leaves, and flowers
Porcelain with underglaze cobalt decoration
8 1/16 in. diam. (20.4 cm.)
Gift of Mrs. Mason Knox, from the Estate of Julia Rogers
BMA 1945.22.30

84
Jiangxi province, Jingdezhen kilns
Ming dynasty, Chongzhen period (1628–1644)
OPENWORK BOWL WITH FLORAL PANELS
(mid-17th century)
Description: pine, bamboo, plum blossoms, chrysanthemum, and orchid
Porcelain with underglaze cobalt decoration
3 3/4 in. diam. (9.5 cm.)
Bequest of Mathilde Whitridge Johnson
BMA 1976.95.5
Provenance: William H. Whitridge, Baltimore

85
Jiangxi province, Jingdezhen kilns
Ming dynasty, Chongzhen period (1628–1644)
BOTTLE VASE
(c. 1635–1645)
Description: flattened round body and long neck with bulb; scene from *The Romance of the Three Kingdoms* on body and tulips on neck
Porcelain with underglaze cobalt decoration
14 1/2 in. high (36.9 cm.)
The George A. Lucas Collection of The Maryland Institute, College of Art, on extended loan to The Baltimore Museum of Art
BMA L.1966.7.33

86
Jiangxi province, Jingdezhen kilns
Qing dynasty, Shunzhi period (1644–1661)
VASE
(c. 1650)
Description: bird sitting on branch
Porcelain with underglaze cobalt decoration
6 7/8 in. high (17.4 cm.)
Frank J. and Elizabeth L. Goodnow Collection
BMA 1942.70.370

87
Jiangxi province, Jingdezhen kilns
Qing dynasty, Kangxi period (1662–1722)
SEAL PASTE BOX DECORATED WITH RIVER SCENE
Description: scholar in pavilion; attendants on bridge
Porcelain with underglaze cobalt decoration
Period character mark (*Wan yu*) on bottom
2 11/16 in. diam. (6.8 cm.)
The Cone Collection, formed by Dr. Claribel Cone and Miss Etta Cone of Baltimore, Maryland
BMA 1950/85.3a-b

88
Jiangxi province, Jingdezhen kilns
Qing dynasty, Kangxi period (1662–1722)
SMALL BRUSH WASHER
Description: two men in a landscape
Porcelain with underglaze cobalt decoration
Period brush, ink cake, and scepter mark on bottom
3 1/8 in. diam. (7.8 cm.)
The Cone Collection, formed by Dr. Claribel Cone and Miss Etta Cone of Baltimore, Maryland
BMA 1950/87.4

89
Jiangxi province, Jingdezhen kilns
Qing dynasty, Kangxi period (1662–1722)
COVERED JAR
Description: geometric medallions
Porcelain with underglaze cobalt decoration
6 5/8 in. high (16.8 cm.)
Bequest of Francis Burns Harvey
BMA 1931.20.51a-b

90
Jiangxi province, Jingdezhen kilns
Qing dynasty, Kangxi period (1662–1722)
PAIR OF COVERED CYLINDRICAL VASES
(c. 1690)
Description: overall stylized chrysanthemum scroll
Porcelain with underglaze cobalt decoration
Period artemisia leaf and ribbon mark in double circle on bottom
7 1/16 in. high (18 cm.), each
Bequest of Francis Burns Harvey
BMA 1931.20.54a-b, 55a-b

91
Jiangxi province, Jingdezhen kilns
Qing dynasty, Kangxi period (1662–1722)
COVERED OVOID JAR
Description: two women arranging and admiring flowers
Porcelain with underglaze cobalt decoration
Period artemisia leaf mark on bottom
11 5/16 in. high (28.8 cm.)
Bequest of Francis Burns Harvey
BMA 1931.20.58a-b

92
Jiangxi province, Jingdezhen kilns
Qing dynasty, Kangxi period (1662–1722)
PEAR-SHAPED VASE WITH HIGH FOOT
Description: interior scenes enclosed within panels
Porcelain with underglaze cobalt decoration
10 1/4 in. high (26 cm.)
Bequest of Francis Burns Harvey
BMA 1931.20.63
Provenance: James A. Garland, New York; J. Pierpont Morgan Collection, New York

93
Jiangxi province, Jingdezhen kilns
Qing dynasty, Kangxi period (1662–1722)
SEAL PASTE BOX
Description: 100 Boys motif
Soft-paste porcelain with underglaze cobalt decoration
Period artemisia leaf mark on bottom
3 7/8 in. diam. (9.9 cm.)
Bequest of Francis Burns Harvey
BMA 1931.20.64a-b

94
Jiangxi province, Jingdezhen kilns
Qing dynasty, Kangxi period (1662–1772)
VASE
Description: floral and foliate design
Porcelain with underglaze cobalt decoration
8 3/8 in. high (21.3 cm.)
Bequest of Francis Burns Harvey
BMA 1931.20.68

95
Jiangxi province, Jingdezhen kilns
Qing dynasty, Kangxi period (1662–1772)
PAIR OF BOTTLE VASES
Description: overall flower-and-vine scroll
Porcelain with underglaze cobalt decoration
Period letter "G" mark on bottom of each
.74) 8 3/16 in. high (19.8 cm.);
.75) 7 1/2 in. high (19 cm.)
Bequest of Francis Burns Harvey
BMA 1931.20.74-75

96
Jiangxi province, Jingdezhen kilns
Qing dynasty, Kangxi period (1662–1772)
PEAR-SHAPED VASE ON HIGH FOOT
Description: panels enclosing interior scenes and objects
Porcelain with underglaze cobalt decoration
10 7/16 in. high (26.5 cm.)
Bequest of Francis Burns Harvey
BMA 1931.20.87
Provenance: James A. Garland, New York; J. Pierpont Morgan Collection, New York

97
Jiangxi province, Jingdezhen kilns
Qing dynasty, Kangxi period (1662–1722)
TWO PEAR-SHAPED VASES ON HIGH FEET
Description: fans on tables; hanging urns
Porcelain with underglaze cobalt decoration
Period flower mark on bottom of each
.88) 10 1/16 in. high (25.6 cm.);
.89) 10 1/4 in. high (26.1 cm.)
Bequest of Francis Burns Harvey
BMA 1931.20.88-89

98
Jiangxi province, Jingdezhen kilns
Qing dynasty, Kangxi period (1662–1722)
TWO CUPS
Description: finely painted dragon medallions
Porcelain with underglaze cobalt decoration
Period 6-character reign mark on bottom of each
3 5/8 in. diam. (9.2 cm.), each
Gift of Lawrason Riggs of J
BMA 1945.59.6.1-2

99
Jiangxi province, Jingdezhen kilns
Qing dynasty, Kangxi period (1662–1722)
BALUSTER JAR
Description: The Eight Immortals
Porcelain with underglaze cobalt decoration
Period double circle mark on bottom
10 1/8 in. high (25.7 cm.)
Gift of Lawrason Riggs of J
BMA 1945.59.35

100
Jiangxi province, Jingdezhen kilns
Qing dynasty, Kangxi period (1662–1722)
TWO COVERED VASES
Description: various landscape scenes
Porcelain with underglaze cobalt decoration
.13a-b) 10 3/8 in. high overall (26.4 cm.);
.14a-b) 10 7/16 in. high overall (26.5 cm.)
Bequest of Mathilde Whitridge Johnson
BMA 1976.95.13a-b, 14a-b
Provenance: William H. Whitridge, Baltimore

101
Jiangxi province, Jingdezhen kilns
Qing dynasty, Kangxi period (1662–1722)
ZUN-SHAPED VASE
Description: scene from a drama
Porcelain with underglaze cobalt decoration
Spurious 6-character Chenghua mark within double circle on bottom
17 in. high (43.1 cm.)
Gift of Mr. and Mrs. Fred J. van Slyke
BMA 1967.68

102
Jiangxi province, Jingdezhen kilns
Qing dynasty, Kangxi period (1662–1722)
JAR
(c. 1680)
Description: two scenes: ox herd and spinning maiden; man with horses beside a river
Porcelain with underglaze cobalt decoration
9 1/16 in. diam. (23 cm.)
The George A. Lucas Collection of The Maryland Institute, College of Art, on extended loan to The Baltimore Museum of Art
BMA L.1966.7.1

103
Jiangxi province, Jingdezhen kilns
Qing dynasty, Kangxi period (1662–1722)
VASE DECORATED WITH SCHOLARS IN A LANDSCAPE SCENE
(c. 1690–1710)
Description: two men conversing on a rocky bank, mountains in the distance
Porcelain with underglaze cobalt decoration
7 3/8 in. high (18.7 cm.)
The George A. Lucas Collection of The Maryland Institute, College of Art, on extended loan to The Baltimore Museum of Art
BMA L.1966.7.16

104
Jiangxi province, Jingdezhen kilns
Qing dynasty, Kangxi period (1662–1722)
COVERED JAR
Description: scene from a drama
Porcelain with underglaze cobalt decoration
Spurious 6-character Chenghua reign mark within double circle on bottom
$7\frac{1}{2}$ in. high (19.1 cm.)
The George A. Lucas Collection of The Maryland Institute, College of Art, on extended loan to The Baltimore Museum of Art
BMA L.1966.7.38a-b

105
Jiangxi province, Jingdezhen kilns
Qing dynasty, Kangxi period (1662–1722)
PLANTER
Description: two men beside a river, waterfall in the background
Porcelain with underglaze cobalt decoration
$9\frac{3}{8}$ in. diam. (23.8 cm.)
The George A. Lucas Collection of The Maryland Institute, College of Art, on extended loan to The Baltimore Museum of Art
BMA L.1966.7.45

106
Jiangxi province, Jingdezhen kilns
Qing dynasty, Kangxi period (1662–1722)
TWO BEAKER VASES
Porcelain with powder blue glaze
Period double circle mark on bottom of each
$7\frac{5}{8}$ in. high (19.3 cm.), each
Frank J. and Elizabeth L. Goodnow Collection
BMA 1942.70.315-316

107
Jiangxi province, Jingdezhen kilns
Qing dynasty, Kangxi period (1662–1722)
VASE
Description: chrysanthemums and a poem in honor of Tao Yuan Ming
Porcelain with powder blue glaze and overglaze gilt decoration
$17\frac{15}{16}$ in. high (45.6 cm.)
The George A. Lucas Collection of The Maryland Institute, College of Art, on extended loan to The Baltimore Museum of Art
BMA L.1966.7.28

108
Jiangxi province, Jingdezhen kilns
Qing dynasty, Kangxi period (1662–1722)
BOTTLE VASE
Description: originally decorated with overglaze gilt dragon design
Porcelain with mirror black glaze
$7\frac{1}{2}$ in. high (19 cm.)
Gift of Lawrason Riggs of J
BMA 1945.59.15

109
Probably Jiangxi province
Qing dynasty, Kangxi period (1662–1722)
WATER DROPPER IN THE FORM OF A BAMBOO SHOOT
(late 17th century)
Description: lizard perched on one side
Porcelain with transparent glaze
$4\frac{5}{8}$ in. long (11.7 cm.)
Gift of Lawrason Riggs of J
BMA 1945.59.33

110
Jiangxi province, Jingdezhen kilns
Qing dynasty, Kangxi period (1662–1722)
BALUSTER VASE
Description: incised and slip-trailed design of bamboo leaves
Porcelain with transparent glaze
Spurious 4-character Hongzhi reign mark
$7\frac{11}{16}$ in. high (19.5 cm.)
Gift of William C. Whitridge, Stevenson, Maryland
BMA 1979.125
Provenance: William H. Whitridge, Baltimore

111
Jiangxi province, Jingdezhen kilns
Qing dynasty, Kangxi period (1662–1722)
TWO BOWLS
Porcelain with oxblood glaze
$4\frac{7}{8}$ in. diam. (12.3 cm.), each
Gift of Lawrason Riggs of J
BMA 1945.59.25.1-2

112
Jiangxi province, Jingdezhen kilns
Qing dynasty, Kangxi period (1662–1722)
BRUSH WASHER
(early 18th century)
Porcelain with peachbloom glaze
Period 6-character Kangxi mark on bottom
$5\frac{1}{16}$ in. diam. (12.8 cm.)
Gift of Terri and Erwin Harris, Baltimore
BMA 1989.368

113
Jiangxi province, Jingdezhen kilns
Qing dynasty, Kangxi period (1662–1722)
WINE CUP
(c. 1665–1675)
Description: domestic scene
Porcelain with overglaze polychrome enamel decoration
Period 4-character reign mark within double circle on bottom
$7\frac{5}{8}$ in. high (19.4 cm.)
The Cone Collection, formed by Dr. Claribel Cone and Miss Etta Cone of Baltimore, Maryland
BMA 1950/85.1

114
Jiangxi province, Jingdezhen kilns
Qing dynasty, Kangxi period (1662–1722)
"TANTALLUS" WINE CUP
Description: leaves surrounding a man
Porcelain with polychrome enamels "on the biscuit"
$3\frac{5}{16}$ in. diam. (8.5 cm.)
Bequest of Mathilde Whitridge Johnson
BMA 1976.95.19
Provenance: William H. Whitridge, Baltimore; James A. Garland Collection, New York; J. Pierpont Morgan Collection, New York

115
Jiangxi province, Jingdezhen kilns
Qing dynasty, Kangxi period (1662–1722)
LARGE BALUSTER VASE
Description: four phoenixes against flower and vine scroll ground
Porcelain with underglaze cobalt and overglaze polychrome enamel decoration
$18\frac{3}{8}$ in. high (46.6 cm.)
Bequest of Mathilde Whitridge Johnson
BMA 1976.95.21
Provenance: Ralph M. Chait, New York

116
Jiangxi province, Jingdezhen kilns
Qing dynasty, Kangxi period (1662–1722)
LARGE BALUSTER VASE
Description: pheasants and flowers
Porcelain with polychrome enamel decoration
$17\frac{5}{8}$ in. high (44.8 cm.)
Bequest of Mathilde Whitridge Johnson
BMA 1976.95.22
Provenance: Ralph M. Chait, New York

117
Jiangxi province, Jingdezhen kilns
Qing dynasty, Kangxi period (1662–1722)
BOWL
Porcelain with polychrome enamels "on the biscuit"
6 15/16 in. diam. (17.7 cm.)
Gift of Janet Longcope
BMA 1946.43

118
Jiangxi province, Jingdezhen kilns
Qing dynasty, Kangxi period (1662–1722)
BOWL
Description: The Eight Immortals in high relief
Earthenware with polychrome enamels "on the biscuit"
4 13/16 in. diam. (12.2 cm.)
The Mary Frick Jacobs Collection
BMA 1940.148.2

119
Jiangxi province, Jingdezhen kilns
Qing dynasty, Yongzheng period (1723–1735)
SMALL PEAR-SHAPED VASE
Porcelain with Longquan-type celadon glaze
6 3/8 in. high overall (16.2 cm.)
Gift of Lawrason Riggs of J
BMA 1945.59.2

120
Jiangxi province, Jingdezhen kilns
Qing dynasty, Qianlong period (1736–1795)
MEIPING VASE
Description: peaches
Porcelain with underglaze cobalt decoration
6 13/16 in. high (17.3 cm.)
Bequest of Francis Burns Harvey
BMA 1931.20.43

121
Jiangxi province, Jingdezhen kilns
Qing dynasty, Qianlong period (1736–1795)
MEIPING VASE
Description: bird beneath a tree
"Huaci" porcelain with underglaze cobalt decoration
5 1/16 in. high (12.8 cm.)
Bequest of Francis Burns Harvey
BMA 1931.20.48

122
Jiangxi province, Jingdezhen kilns
Qing dynasty, Qianlong period (1736–1795)
VASE
Description: man sitting in a tree
"Huaci" porcelain with underglaze cobalt decoration
Spurious 4-character Chenghua mark on bottom
5 1/2 in. high (14 cm.)
Bequest of Francis Burns Harvey
BMA 1931.20.70

123
Jiangxi province, Jingdezhen kilns
Qing dynasty, Qianlong period (1736–1795)
THREE VASES
Description: deer, pine, mushroom, and bat
"Huaci" porcelain with underglaze cobalt decoration
.71) 7 5/8 in. high (19.4 cm.);
.72) 7 1/2 in. high (19.1 cm.);
.73) 7 1/4 in. high (18.5 cm.)
Bequest of Francis Burns Harvey
BMA 1931.20.71-73

124
Jiangxi province, Jingdezhen kilns
Qing dynasty, Qianlong period (1736–1795)
LARGE TOU-HU SHAPED VASE
Description: lotus scroll
Porcelain with underglaze cobalt decoration
Period 6-character Qianlong seal script mark on bottom
22 11/16 in. high (57.6 cm.)
Frank J. and Elizabeth L. Goodnow Collection
BMA 1942.70.420

125
Jiangxi province, Jingdezhen kilns
Qing dynasty, Qianlong period (1736–1795)
LARGE VASE (CUT-DOWN NECK)
Description: lotus flowers, lilies of the valley, and beads
Porcelain with underglaze cobalt decoration
Period 6-character reign mark within double circle on bottom
22 1/16 in. high (56 cm.)
Gift of Alfred R. and Henry G. Riggs, in Memory of General Lawrason Riggs
BMA 1941.197
Provenance: General Lawrason Riggs

126
Jiangxi province, Jingdezhen kilns
Qing dynasty, Qianlong period (1736–1795)
VASE
Porcelain with oxblood glaze
13 5/16 in. high (33.8 cm.)
Gift of Lawrason Riggs of J
BMA 1945.59.27

127
Jiangxi province, Jingdezhen kilns
Qing dynasty, Qianlong period (1736–1795)
VASE
Porcelain with oxblood glaze
Underglaze incised mark (*tian*) on bottom
8 15/16 in. high (22.7 cm.)
Gift of Lawrason Riggs of J
BMA 1945.59.31

128
Jiangxi province, Jingdezhen kilns
Qing dynasty, Qianlong period (1736–1795)
SMALL MEIPING VASE
Porcelain with Guan-type celadon glaze
4 3/4 in. high (12.1 cm.)
Bequest of Mathilde Whitridge Johnson
BMA 1976.95.20
Provenance: William H. Whitridge, Baltimore

129
Jiangxi province, Jingdezhen kilns
Qing dynasty, Qianlong period (1736–1795)
SQUARE VASE WITH FIVE MOUTHS
Porcelain with imitation Song dynasty Ru-type glaze
10 3/8 in. high (26.3 cm.)
Period 6-character seal script reign mark on bottom
The George A. Lucas Collection of The Maryland Institute, College of Art, on extended loan to The Baltimore Museum of Art
BMA L.1966.7.42

130
Jiangxi province, Jingdezhen kilns
Qing dynasty, Qianlong period (1736–1795)
RECTANGULAR DOUBLE-GOURD VASE
Porcelain with Ru-type celadon glaze
Period 4-character seal script reign mark on bottom
5 1/8 in. high (13 cm.)
Gift of William C. Whitridge, Stevenson, Maryland
BMA 1979.129
Provenance: William H. Whitridge, Baltimore

131
Jiangxi province, Jingdezhen kilns
Qing dynasty, Qianlong period (1736–1795)
PAIR OF LARGE COVERED VASES
Description: phoenixes, rockwork, and flowering peony and magnolia trees
Porcelain with overglaze iron red, pink, turquoise, yellow, green, blue, and black enamels
52 3/16 in. high (132.5 cm.)
Gift of Arthur A. Houghton, Jr., Queenstown, Maryland
BMA 1987.213.1-2
Provenance: Parke-Bernet, New York, 1958; Mrs. R. B. Astley, Acton Reynold Hall, Shropshire; Edward T. Stotesbury, Philadelphia; Mrs. Eva R. Stotesbury, Palm Beach; Duveen Brothers, New York

132
Fujian province, Dehua kilns
Qing dynasty (1644–1911)
MILO (THE BUDDHA OF THE FUTURE)
(18th–19th century)
Porcelain with transparent glaze
Underglaze incised mark (*mu*) in interior
5 15/16 in. high (15 cm.)
Gift of Lawrason Riggs of J
BMA 1945.59.9

133
Fujian province, Dehua kilns
Qing dynasty (1644–1911)
BUDDAI
(18th century)
Porcelain with transparent glaze
4 5/16 in. wide (11 cm.)
Gift of Lawrason Riggs of J
BMA 1945.59.10

134
Fujian province, Dehua kilns
Qing dynasty (1644–1911)
CYLINDRICAL VASE
(19th century)
Description: sprig-molded lotus flowers around side
Porcelain with transparent glaze
6 7/8 in. high (17.5 cm.)
Gift of Lawrason Riggs of J
BMA 1945.59.30a-b

135
Jiangxi province, Jingdezhen kilns
Qing dynasty, Jiaqing period (1796–1820)
LARGE HU-SHAPED VASE
(early 19th century)
Porcelain with tea dust glaze
15 5/16 in. high (38.9 cm.)
Frank J. and Elizabeth L. Goodnow Collection
BMA 1942.70.301

136
Jiangxi province, Jingdezhen kilns
Qing dynasty (1644–1911)
ALTAR SET
(early 19th century)
Description: impressed overall geometric motif with lingzhi fungus and peaches against a diaper ground
Porcelain with bright green enamel "on the biscuit"
.1a-b) covered censer: 14 15/16 in. high (38 cm.); .2-3) vases: 13 in. high (33 cm.), each; .4-5) candlesticks: 13 3/16 in. high (33.4 cm.), each
Gift of William C. Whitridge, Stevenson, Maryland
BMA 1979.122.1-5
Provenance: William H. Whitridge, Baltimore

137
Jiangxi province, Jingdezhen kilns
Qing dynasty (1644–1911)
GUI-SHAPED INCENSE BURNER
(19th century)
Description: elephant-head handles
Porcelain with turquoise enamel glaze
9 5/8 in. spread (24.5 cm.)
Gift of Fred J. van Slyke
BMA 1965.41.3

138
Jiangxi province, Jingdezhen kilns
Qing dynasty (1644–1911)
CONG-SHAPED VASE
(early 19th century)
Porcelain with turquoise enamel glaze
11 in. high (28 cm.)
The George A. Lucas Collection of The Maryland Institute, College of Art, on extended loan to The Baltimore Museum of Art
BMA L.1966.7.46

139
Jiangxi province, Jingdezhen kilns
Qing dynasty (1644–1911)
HU-SHAPED VASE
(early 19th century)
Description: dragon faces
Porcelain with underglaze cobalt decoration
15 3/16 in. high (38.5 cm.)
The George A. Lucas Collection of The Maryland Institute, College of Art, on extended loan to The Baltimore Museum of Art
BMA L.1966.7.7

140
Jiangxi province, Jingdezhen kilns
Qing dynasty (1644–1911)
HU-SHAPED VASE
(c. 1850)
Description: dragons, bats, and peaches of immortality
Porcelain with underglaze cobalt decoration
12 3/16 in. high (31 cm.)
Frank J. and Elizabeth L. Goodnow Collection
BMA 1942.70.369

141
Jiangxi province, Jingdezhen kilns
Qing dynasty (1644–1911)
HU-SHAPED VASE
(19th century)
Porcelain with monochrome (copper flambé) glaze
11 11/16 in. high (29.7 cm.)
The George A. Lucas Collection of The Maryland Institute, College of Art, on extended loan to The Baltimore Museum of Art
BMA L.1966.7.29

142
Guangdong province, Guangzhou (Canton), Shiwan ware
Qing dynasty (1644–1911)
RAM VASE
(late 19th century)
Stoneware with Jun-type glaze
7 3/16 in. high (18.2 cm.)
Julius Levy Memorial Fund
BMA 1939.236
Provenance: William H. Whitridge, Baltimore

143
Jiangsu province, I-xing potteries
Qing dynasty (1644–1911)
GROUP OF FRUITS, NUTS, AND SEEDS
Stoneware with various colored slips
.a) walnut: 1 3/8 in. long (3.5 cm.);
.b) sunflower seed: 13/16 in. long (2 cm.);
.c) chestnut: 1 3/8 in. long (3.5 cm.);
.d) ovoid nut: 1 1/8 in. long (2.8 cm.);
.e) caltrop: 3 1/16 in. long (7.8 cm.);
.f) peanut: 1 1/2 in. long (3.9 cm.);
.g) round fruit: 1 3/8 in. diam. (3.5 cm.);
.h) melon seed: 1 1/16 in. long (1.7 cm.);
.i) lotus bulb: 3 1/16 in. long (7.8 cm.)
Gift of Terri and Erwin Harris, Baltimore
BMA 1988.159a-i

SELECTED REFERENCES

Bickford, Maggie. *Bones of Jade, Soul of Ice: The Flowering Plum in Chinese Art.* New Haven: Yale University Art Gallery, 1985.

Chang, Kwang-chih. *The Archaeology of Ancient China.* 4th ed. New Haven and London: Yale University Press, 1986.

Eberhard, Wolfram. *A Dictionary of Chinese Symbols: Hidden Symbols in Chinese Life and Thought.* Translated by G. L. Campbell. London: Routledge, 1986.

Fitzgerald, C. P. *The Horizon History of China.* New York: American Heritage Publishing Co., Inc., 1969.

Fontein, Jan, and Wu Tung. *The World's Great Collections: Oriental Ceramics.* Museum of Fine Arts, Boston, vol. 10. Tokyo, New York, and San Francisco: Kodansha International Ltd., 1980.

Gompertz, G. St. G. M. *Chinese Celadon Wares.* Rev. ed. London and Boston: Faber and Faber Ltd., 1980.

Gray, Basil. *Sung Porcelain and Stoneware.* London: Faber and Faber, 1984.

Hughes-Stanton, Penelope, and Rose Kerr. *Kiln Sites of Ancient China.* London: Oriental Ceramic Society, 1980.

Iron in the Fire: The Chinese Potters' Exploration of Iron Oxide Glazes. London: The Oriental Ceramic Society, 1988.

Jacobsen, Robert D. "Ceramic Tomb Sets of Early Tang." *Minneapolis Institute of Arts Bulletin* 64 (1978–1980): 5–23.

Juliano, Annette. *Bronze, Clay and Stone: Chinese Art in the C. C. Wang Family Collection.* Seattle: University of Washington Press, 1988.

Kerr, Rose. *Chinese Ceramics: Porcelain of the Qing Dynasty 1644–1911.* London: Victoria and Albert Museum, 1986.

Lee, George J. *Selected Far Eastern Art in the Yale University Art Gallery.* New Haven and London: Yale University Press, 1970.

Lewis, Candace J. *Into the Afterlife: Han and Six Dynasties Chinese Tomb Sculpture from the Schloss Collection.* Poughkeepsie, New York: Vassar College Art Gallery, 1990.

Lim, Lucy. *Stories from China's Past: Han Dynasty Pictorial Tomb Reliefs and Archaeological Objects from Sichuan Province, People's Republic of China.* San Francisco: The Chinese Culture Foundation of San Francisco, 1987.

Lion-Goldschmidt, Daisy. *Ming Porcelain.* Translated by Katherine Watson. New York: Rizzoli, 1978.

Little, Stephen. *Chinese Ceramics of the Transitional Period: 1620–1683.* New York: China Institute in America, 1983.

Lu Yaw. *Song Ceramics.* Singapore: Southeast Asian Ceramic Society, 1983.

Medley, Margaret. *Yüan Porcelain and Stoneware.* London: Faber and Faber, 1974.

Mino, Yutaka. *Freedom of Clay and Brush through Seven Centuries in Northern China: Tz'u-chou Type Wares, 960–1600 A.D.* Indianapolis: Indianapolis Museum of Art, 1980.

Mino, Yutaka, and Katherine R. Tsiang. *Ice and Green Clouds: Traditions of Chinese Celadon.* Indianapolis: Indianapolis Museum of Art, Indiana University Press, 1986.

Pirazzoli-t'Serstevens, Michèle. *The Han Dynasty.* Translated by Janet Seligman. New York: Rizzoli, 1982.

Powers, Martin Joseph. "The Shapes of Power in Han Pictorial Art." Ph.D. dissertation, University of Chicago, 1978.

The Quest for Eternity. Los Angeles: Los Angeles County Museum of Art, Chronicle Books, 1987.

Rawson, Jessica. *Chinese Ornament: The Lotus and the Dragon.* New York: Holmes and Meier, 1984.

Riddell, Sheila. *Dated Chinese Antiquities: 600–1650.* London and Boston: Faber and Faber, 1979.

Schafer, Edward H. *The Golden Peaches of Samarkand: A Study of T'ang Exotics.* 1963. Reprint. Berkeley: University of California Press, 1985.

Shangraw, Clarence F. *Origins of Chinese Ceramics.* New York: China Institute in America, Inc., 1978.

Tang. London: Eskenazi, 1987.

Tregear, Mary. *Song Ceramics.* New York: Rizzoli, 1982.

Valenstein, Suzanne G. *A Handbook of Chinese Ceramics.* 2d ed., rev. New York: The Metropolitan Museum of Art, 1989.

Wang Zhongshu. *Han Civilization.* Translated by K. C. Chang and Collaborators. New Haven and London: Yale University Press, 1982.

Watson, William. *Tang and Liao Ceramics.* New York: Rizzoli, 1984.